Be The Human Sunshine

CLARE BOSTOCK

PRAISE FOR *BE THE HUMAN SUNSHINE*

This book is the perfect blend of *inspiration*, aspiration, positivity and hope – and a must for anyone who wants to make a difference in their life. Clare's wisdom, and absolute *authenticity* is a refreshing gift that is packaged perfectly to assist in bringing about the reader's highest vision into fruition, and to shine their light brightly as they take charge of their own destiny.

FLAVIA KATE PETERS
BEST SELLING AUTHOR OF
WAY OF THE FAERY SHAMAN

❧

Be the Human Sunshine is a *thought-provoking* book and exercise in the art of journaling – bringing to light its many benefits, from getting to know oneself on a deeper level, to leaving behind a chronicle of one's thoughts and experiences for future generations. It contains a *wealth of practical guidance* as well as reflections on life that will appeal to both novices and experienced writers alike.

ALISON KENNEY
ENTERTAINMENT ONE LICENSING

My journey began at the airport, I had waited so long to to commence my trip to see my daughter in Dubai. Then, suddenly! I was immersed so unexpectedly into my own little world. I found peace and *tranquility* from the first page of *Be the Human Sunshine*, my soul began to dance with calmness and happiness, lost on another journey I did not expect. I was disturbed by my tears of joy, feeling blessed and privileged to be part of *Be the Human Sunshine...* My Morning Jottings and Scrolls have already begun to unfold in such a short period of time, any negative thoughts I have are dismissed and put into my Pickle Jar, filtering out of my head space. I feel at *peace* and look forward to my future with the *Be the Human Sunshine* in my life, also inspiring others through my work, I feel blessed and privileged to endorse this book, thank you so much Clare.

KAREN NICHOLSON
INDEPENDENT DOMESTIC VIOLENCE ADVISOR

❧

Clare speaks from her heart and shares wonderful words of wisdom that you can take with you wherever you go. This book is a real *ray of sunshine* that will light up your life.

BARBARA MEIKLEJOHN-FREE
BEST SELLING & AWARD WINNING AUTHOR
OF *THE SHAMAN WITHIN*
& *THE HEART OF ALL KNOWING*

Matador
9 Priory Business Park,
Wistow Road, Kibworth Beauchamp,
Leicestershire. LE8 0RX
Tel: (+44) 116 279 2299
Fax: (+44) 116 279 2277
Email: books@troubador.co.uk
Web: www.troubador.co.uk/matador

ISBN 978 1784620 318

British Library Cataloguing in Publication Data.
A catalogue record for this book is available from the British Library.

Typeset in 11pt Bembo by Troubador Publishing Ltd, Leicester, UK

Matador is an imprint of Troubador Publishing Ltd

I dedicate this journ-book collection to my children
Sean and *Ethan* you are both where my sun rises and sets.
I hope I have and will continue to make you proud
live your dreams the world is yours.
Always, Mumma, Mummy, Mum, Mother – Peg x

To You
Books are the destination and the journey. They are
home. Without leaps of imagination or dreaming, we
lose the excitement and thrill of all present and future
possibilities and adventures. Dreaming is a form of
planning; dream like the child with your eyes open and
write the book you want to be written, a journal full of
portable, memorable and possible magic."

To God, the beloved great mystery
Your effulgence has lit a fire in my heart.
My whole life I have heard your voice and daily I have
entered into quiet conversation with you.
As I listened, you gently whispered the words *"Do not be
satisfied with others stories you must unfold your own."*
Forever, I have been searching for your face and there in
the blankness *I felt it..... I found it.....*
Picking up my pen I wove the colours of my soul and
began to write this book.
C.B

CONTENTS

ACKNOWLEDGEMENTS

J would like to express my deepest gratitude to the many people who saw me through this journ-book collection; to all those who provided support, listened to the many drafts, talked things over, read, offered comments, allowed me to quote and assisted in the editing, proofreading and design.

Firstly, my deepest thanks and gratitude to the wonderfully talented, world famous fantasy artist Josephine Wall, it is an honour to have your illustrations included in my books. My collection would not have been what I envisioned from cover to end without them; your paintings are the *spine* of my books and were my inspiration when I felt like giving up. Gratitude to Alison Kenney, Entertainment One Los Angeles, Josephine's agent, for your kindness in authorizing and licensing all of my requests, I am deeply grateful. Josephine's art gallery can be viewed on her website at www.josephinewall.co.uk.

Above all, I want to thank my husband, John, and children, Sean and Ethan (*everything I do is because of, and for you. Do not be afraid to live your dreams and never let anyone tell you, you can't, you can*) who supported and encouraged me, in spite of all the times my *page adventures* took me away from them, enabling me to fulfil my life-long dream. My parents Kay and Gerard, my message is because of you, and the way I was raised, thank you. Also my brothers Greg and Gerard who have always believed in me, it was a long and difficult journey, but I, we did it... I hope I have, and will continue to make you proud. *You are my world. I love you all. Here is to a God wink moment!* To those of my family who have passed "I miss you" and present, I love you all. Thank you for your gift of love and human sunshine, you are all forever in my heart.

Barbara Meiklejohn-Free, Seer, Shaman, High Priestess and Elder, without your guidance and words this book would have not been written, eternally grateful, forever my friend. Flavia Kate-Peters *Way of the Faery Shaman* you are both the essence of human sunshine.

I would like to thank Jeremy Thompson, Jessica Hutchinson, Alice Graham, Rosie Grindrod and Naomi Green for helping me in the process of selection and editing. Thanks to my publisher Matador and the team for enabling me to publish this book, you have all been so patient, kind and understanding. Amy Kiberd at Hay House London for your encouragement, guidance and listening ear, many blessings always.

My friends and colleagues at Local Solutions, for the countless hours I ran ideas passed you and you so patiently listened and encouraged me, thank you. For every disadvantaged young adult I have had the pleasure to meet and work with from the United Kingdom and around the world, who allowed me to participate in and be touched by your human sunshine, it was, and continues to be a privilege.

Willy Russell, for his kind words in a letter comparing me to great writers of Liverpool over eight years ago, I read and re-read in awe that I had received a letter from you, you are a legend. I know all dreams can be achieved if you believe in yourself, but you must reach out into the limitless. I am proud to be a scouser.

Last and not least: God, the Divine, beloved, great mystery, thank you for holding me and in you I have every faith. You are the music of my soul, I take your hand again and again.

I acknowledge you, my readers, may you find comfort in this book and long may you give and receive the gift of human sunshine. I offer you an open invitation to the greatest dance of all "*life*", here comes the first beat. Will you dance with me? You must be willing to accept the dance to awaken the dream.

I ask forgiveness of all those who have been with me over the course of the years and whose names I have failed to mention. I can be contacted on my official Twitter page

@sunshinescrolls also, Be the Human Sunshine Community, Facebook. I look forward to meeting you all at my "*Letters from Juliet*" writing to heal workshops this year. Remember! All will come together where life is a song and those are human sunshine.

Delivering human sunshine always,

Clare

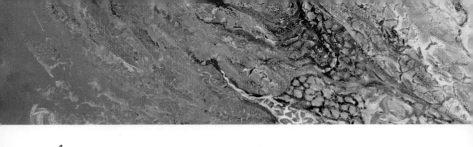

"Life is an opportunity, benefit from it.

Life is beauty, admire it.

Life is a dream, realise it.

Life is a challenge, meet it.

Life is a duty, complete it.

Life is a game, play it.

Life is a promise, fulfil it.

Life is sorrow, overcome it.

Life is a song, sing it.

Life is a struggle, accept it.

Life is a tragedy, confront it.

Life is an adventure, dare it.

Life is luck, make it.

Life is too precious, do not destroy it.

Life is life, fight for it."

MOTHER TERESA OF CALCUTTA

(26 August 1910 – 5 September 1997)

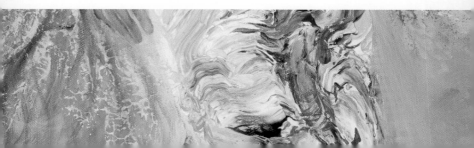

The Message

"LET US ALL BE CALLED TO MAKE LIFE
BEAUTIFUL, SIMPLY – BY BEING HUMAN."

SUNSHINE SCROLLS

"Human sunshine has the power to change anything..."

Welcome to *Be the Human Sunshine* "Little Journ-book of Something". It is my hope that you live in the spirit of this beautiful message; to be a living example of these wonderful words and to understand its simple, inspiring philosophy and basic life-rules; using them in your everyday life.

Human sunshine has the power to change anything, transform anything, heal anything, restoring peace and happiness, causing friendships and relationships to become as beautiful as sunshine itself. Hold faith, throw caution to the wind, be fearless and enter into those darkened places, removing you from the shadow of yourself that keeps you hidden.

Life let it be.

Sometimes; when we reflect on the past and have gratitude for the present and the privilege of living, when appreciating nature or realising the diversity and beauty of the human spirit – human sunshine, suddenly; an ordinary day becomes the extraordinary. We are awoken to moments of real grace and simple understanding. Something inside us stirs. Often, these moments have a temporary, larger than life perspective. Don't let them slip away. *Note them – then journal.*

The Calling

AUTHOR NOTE

*"Remember! No one is perfect,
life is not perfect..."*

Tell me what you ache for? Would you risk it all for the adventure of being alive? My purpose is to help you tap into the healing power of journaling, to journey home to yourself, to accept your inner calling, reduce stress, and to honour the unique story in your own life and work. Journaling is not for those who regularly avoid the whispered longings of their own heart and soul, but for those who care to embrace the constant abundance and renewal from inner-self as well as from universal source energy. Some points or references throughout the book use the words Divine Creator, mystery, beloved or God – please be open-minded.

I am passionate about the power of writing to heal and transform individuals, communities and the world in which we live. This journ-book (I have decided to call them journ-books, due to the content within each of them), the first from my collection, is an open window into the healing power of writing, and serves as a corridor to starting and/or deepening your own reflective writing practice. I believe magical things can happen when spaces are provided for people to write, and they are to be nurtured in that writing. I believe something wonderful can happen when taking a leap of faith into these spaces, whether young or old. I know this to be true.

This journ-book holds within it the greatest secret to life, yet no secret at all (a little love, kindness, compassion, empathy, forgiveness, dignity, acceptance, faith and a whole lot of common sense). Some written jottings and scrolls may be deep and spiritual, others light-hearted and humorous. Some pieces long and other pieces short. That is my intention. All of the pieces fit together in the end. They will help you face the day with a positive breeze and navigate your way successfully through life; no matter what arises on your journey. Within it are simple rules that will help reduce stress, give you a positive outlook, and encourage you to set your own standards and goals. These rules are a simple guide, and you can adapt or add to them. Without basic rules we get lost in the life-sea, and with them we get safely back to shore. By using the simple rules as a spiritual compass we reflect, dock, refuel and set sail again.

Remember! No one is perfect, life is not perfect. I want you to all cling to your imperfections, they are what make you unique, and know that you as a unique being have but one time upon this earth. Never again will such a phenomenal, beautiful, unique person as you be put together a second time around. You have only one chance. Be yourself. Be boundless ocean. Be sky. Be beyond. Go beyond all that is you. Do not postpone life.

Did you know there is a light in this world, a healing spirit more powerful than any darkness we may encounter and we sometimes lose sight of this light when we get lost among suffering, brokenness, sorrow, or too much pain. Then; unexpectedly, the spirit will emerge through the lives of ordinary people who hear a call and answer in extraordinary ways with inspiring acts of compassion, empathy, forgiveness, love and kindness to all. Each of us are called to be a light to others, the light is generated when we are true to our calling in life. And when each of us develops the talents that are part and parcel of our calling, the sunbeam we share ignites the world.

We become co-creators with the Divine – the great mystery. How do we do this? Through the action of spirit, the spirit resides in all of us. The spirit is the Divine Creator's work in and through us. The more we open ourselves to the movement of Divine spirit within – the brighter we shine. We illuminate. We become the roaming, reflecting, travelling and anointing human sunbeam. The Divine Creator wants us to create; he wants us all to shine. This first journ-book is dedicated to you.

May this journaling experience expand you to the farthest edges of the universe; and your heart be opened to receive the mystery. Allow the Beloved to breathe the fragrance of love into your soul; as he has mine.

Blessings Clare

Journaling

THE BASICS

I understand many of you may not have used a journal before, therefore I have laid out the basics of journaling for you. This journal holds, through its jottings (writings), continual prompts from title to verse, exercises to tasks. It also prompts you to get into the habit of journaling in a separate notebook. I will be creating a special notes and jottings book in the collection to accompany all journbooks called *Sunshine Jottings & Scrolls*. You can use this notebook to reflect in and write about anything that inspires you: quotes, art, poetry, affirmations, images, people etc.

In writing in a separate notebook you can add colour, pictures, photographs, postcards and drawings to reflect on your life so far. I had specifically chosen not to create this journal in a way that would merely prompt you to answer questions like: What is your favourite colour, who is your best friend etc. I wanted to go deeper than that, into the parts of yourself that you didn't know were holding on and

"The purpose of journaling is to develop greater understanding..."

preventing you from living fully. I carefully placed specific pieces into separate journals in the collection as I feel this is where they belong, not just in this first journal. Here goes!

Journaling is the act of writing first and foremost for yourself, you write to observe, know, grow and care for yourself by going to the blank page with an open mind, compassionate heart and courageous spirit. The purpose of journaling is to develop greater understanding and awareness of self, others and the world – a journal is your story, the art of you.

Moments captured and shared through stories are all that will survive of us: the stories of who we are recited as people speak our names and remember something we did, an act of kindness or compassion, or an event we lived through, a memory or, hopefully, some wisdom.

There are many ways, in addition to writing, to leave a legacy of story: through photographs, pictures, collage, scrapbooking, poetry, doodling or art. Not everyone has the desire to write, though if you are reading this book – I guess? I hope? – you are willing to give it a try at least. You may have already used a journal or diaries, if you write letters, blog, send personal emails or annotate pictures then you already have treasure to give.

If you were to take those treasures and cultivate them into written vignettes or mini-stories of meaningful events in your life, then you have a say in how those stories are presented. Don't worry about being "not a good enough writer" or "not interesting enough", or think that no one would want to read what you have written. Your stories are more valuable than possessions, or money. Through writing, you leave a gift, a legacy of story that will remain for those you care about and love, for succeeding generations. You will provide an intimate view of your past as presented by your unique personality, your "inner-sunbeam". Without story, the remnants of our ordinary lives quickly lose significance and preciousness.

Today's story is
  tomorrow's history;
    don't let the world
      lose yours.

BENEFITS OF JOURNALING

*J*ournaling can be a life-changing spiritual tool! In the same way you seek a therapist, counsellor or friend to listen to your dilemmas, problems, worries, sorrows or joy, we can listen intently to ourselves. We can do our own inner probing, not that a journal should replace a therapist or counsellor for some, but it could be a nice supplement. When writing in a journal we take a deep dive into our minds, heart and soul. It's a powerful, eye opening practice. Here are just some of the benefits of journaling:

Clarify your thoughts and feelings:

Do you ever seem all jumbled up inside, unsure of what you want or feel? Taking a few minutes to jot down your thoughts and emotions (no editing!) will quickly get you in touch with your internal world.

"Life is a book, you are its author..."

Know yourself better:

By writing routinely you will get to know what makes
you feel happy and confident. You will also become clear
about situations and people who are toxic for you
– important information for your emotional well-being.

Reduce stress:

Writing about anger, sadness, grief and other painful
emotions helps to release the intensity of these feelings.
By doing so you will feel calmer and better able to stay in
the present.

Solve problems more effectively:

Typically we problem solve from a left-brained, analytical
perspective. But sometimes the answer can only be found
by engaging right-brained creativity and intuition. Writing
unlocks these other capabilities, and affords the opportunity
for unexpected solutions to seemingly unsolvable problems.

Resolve disagreements with others:

Writing about misunderstandings rather than stewing over
them will help you to understand another's point of view.
And you just may come up with a sensible resolution
to the conflict.

❧ ⚬ ❧

Making sense of it all:

Sometimes life just doesn't seem to make sense. Bad
things happen to good people and good things happen
to people who don't seem to deserve it. But if we record
our inner perceptions, our honest truths, while moving
through these events, we will not only emerge more
intact and healthy, we reveal treasure chests full of
valuable insights and gifts that we may turn around and
offer others in our lives.

❧ ⚬ ❧

In addition to all of these wonderful benefits, keeping a
journal allows you to track patterns, trends and improvement
and growth over time. When current circumstances appear
insurmountable, you will be able to look back on previous
dilemmas that you have since resolved.

TOOLS OF
THE JOURNAL KEEPER

*P*ens, pencils, crayons, chalks or felt–tips, eraser, glue stick: what you write (or draw) with is as important as the journal you select.

Separate notebook: purchase a separate notebook for your Morning Jottings & Scrolls. Use this for the morning jotting pages only.

Name your journal: as well as naming my writing tools (my sunshine scrollers) I also name my journal. This adds personality to my writings and intimacy with a paper friend.

Sunshine in a Bottle and Pickle Jar: later on in your journal I prompt you to spend some time alone. During this exercise I would like you to purchase a beautiful, coloured glass bottle

"Be grateful for both the positives and negatives in your life..."

and a glass jar (you can use a coloured wine bottle or a jam jar if you wish to save money). For this little "me time" I want you to prepare. Imagine you're going shopping for a new outfit, or a pair of shoes. You would take time buying both wouldn't you? Therefore, choosing/purchasing these two important items for your journaling experience is no different.

You will name the bottle "Sunshine in a Bottle" and the jar "Pickle Jar". As you journal along with life, you will use both of these items to keep or let go of the positives and negatives in your life. As you journey journal, put all of your hopes, dreams and wishes or anything positive that inspires you (quotes, images etc) into your Sunshine in a Bottle; any of the negative stuff/clutter you need to let go of goes into your Pickle Jar. You will notice in time all of the positive things in your life far outweigh the negative.

As a *Be the Human Sunshine* Journal Keeper I offer you this important advice: your Pickle Jar may fill to the brim with all of the negative things in your life you are hoping to let go of – that is the intention, a positive. While the Sunshine in a Bottle may only be half full, you can view this as a cause for optimism (half full) or with a view of pessimism (half empty). I suggest you always see this as a cause for optimism. What is your view? Be grateful for both the positives and negatives in your life, without both of them you could not learn or grow.

Place your Sunshine in a Bottle in a place that inspires you, maybe in your creative, journaling space. You could place your Pickle Jar there also, I often find when I put them together both encourage me. I visually see all of the negative things (pain, sorrow, betrayal, non-forgiveness etc.) I have been able to let go of. This inspires me to journey further, I congratulate myself and give a little pat to the "Angel and Owl on my shoulders" and I never forget to say

"Thank you".

THE MOST IMPORTANT
TOOLS OF A
BE THE HUMAN SUNSHINE
JOURNAL KEEPER

*M*orning Jottings & Scrolls are journaling pages that map the interior self. In order to retrieve all that holds you back from life: your dreams, goals, desires, ambitions and sense of inner you – you at first need to search for and find it! I prompt you to do this by a process called Morning Jottings & Scrolls. To put it simply; three pages of longhand writing, strictly your stream-of-consciousness, mental pen to paper, morning thoughts that drain the brain from negativity. Although occasionally colourful, jottings are often negative, disjointed, worrying, sad, self-pitying, repetitive, boring, angry, joyous or chaotic. Excellent! You have accepted the mission.

"The most important principle is let yourself write..."

Your best journal jottings are done on the mornings when you feel everything isn't going to plan. Or, you are feeling just plain tired or distracted by the many commitments and worries that race through your head. These jottings help you release the stresses of everyday life onto paper. The most important principle is let yourself write... Allow the jottings to teach you what it is that prevents you from moving forward, from appreciating a day well lived, from simply being and holding you back from free-falling into the privilege that is life.

Nobody will see your Morning Jottings so write freely, and nobody is allowed to read them except you; unless you wish to share them at some point in your life. You shouldn't even read them over for the first twelve weeks. Morning Jottings & Scrolls are non-negotiable. So, no excuses! Never skip writing the jottings; your mood doesn't matter. If you don't have time, make time. Begin your first Morning Jottings in this journal and continue writing them in a separate notebook. I am conscious that there is not enough relevant space to write a whole lot in this journal but you can use the prompts from this journal, as a guide, a corridor that leads to life-long journaling. If you're like me, I sometimes cannot think of anything concrete to write, suddenly, something ignites my creative spark then I can't stop. That's why it's important to purchase a separate notebook – the secret here is: I prompt you to get creative throughout your whole journaling experience. Dig deep. You may just find the therapeutic artist in you! Create your own cover for your notebook, you can use: crafts, fabrics, paint, doodle, shade, crayon and felt-tip on your pages. Some beautiful art journaling pages can be found on Pinterest and my friend Karenika's website at www.karenika.com.

Ok! You have carefully selected your notebook — name it Morning Jottings & Scrolls and write only your Morning Jottings in it. Nothing else. Write three pages every day (if you can't think of anything to write — write "I cannot think of anything to write" until you have filled the whole three pages. You will often find you just begin writing. The creative spark ignites, you strike a chord and the music begins. Write anything that comes to mind. Anything. No limits). Tear them out if you wish and pop them into an envelope, adding dates to the top of the pages. You must not read these jottings for twelve weeks.

I will set you journal prompts in this journal for Morning Jottings check in. I am trusting that you will give these "brain drain" pages a try at least. In completing your Morning Jottings & Scrolls you are sending all of your dreams, goals and desires out into the universe. You are also notifying yourself and the Beloved of your fears, dissatisfactions, dilemmas, worries, stresses and problems. Hold faith, all will be listened to, answered and held.

What's the *big deal* of Morning Jottings & Scrolls? The big deal is — take out your jotting notes in twelve weeks and see how much you've changed. It is quite incredible! Many people use this technique in different ways around the world as an important part of their everyday spiritual and therapeutic practice. They never go a day without completing their morning pages and have done so for many years. I was inspired to create the Morning Jottings & Scrolls technique as well as the Juliet Date after reading and using *The Artist's Way* by Julia Cameron.

"Thank you".

JULIET EFFECT –
REFLECTIVE JOURNAL
PRACTICE

*O*nce a week, every week, I want you to go on a "Juliet Date". You are probably saying, "Joking right?" All jokes aside, I'm one hundred percent serious. What is a Juliet Date? A block of time, two hours weekly, set aside for you and your inner-creative-self, the real you. The date is "scroll-play-time-me-time" without the interference of anyone, not your children, family, friends, not even your Romeo! You can't afford any distractions. You spend quality time with your children, family, friends, colleagues and Romeo! But rarely, if you're truly honest, do you ever spend quality time with yourself. Am I right? I can feel you agreeing! You bet I am! Do you ever have fun with yourself? Go on dates? I bet you don't. I can understand the thought of "going it alone" scares the hell out of you, doesn't it? Are you a little reluctant? Frightened? Feel silly? But just as much as it is frightening and silly, a Juliet Date is also remarkably productive. Your inner creativity needs pampering (just as much as your children, friends and your Romeo) nurturing and attention. You don't have to go anywhere extravagant, or go to any great expense, you can sit under a tree at the park, go for a quiet, reflective walk along the beach, have a coffee at a cafe or sit in a quiet room. You choose. Spending time amidst the silence and solitude is essential to self-nurturing. Commit to your Juliet Date and watch how you try to get out of it! You will make every excuse under the sun, moon and the stars not to go "I don't have the time, not enough money, the children need… Romeo needs…" or someone will try and steal your alone time from you or wish to assist. It's not the prom. You can go it alone, no sidekick needed. You have to be tough when the "Time Invaders" step in.

You will try to avoid the date, especially if you are going through a tough time at home or work. We often avoid what the inner-self is telling us, we're scared of the "truth whisperers" within. They could well be saying, "Get rid of Romeo!" Joking! Not. You'd be surprised. Self-disclosure is true intimacy with self. In order to listen to the inner-self we need space and time to listen, to cultivate what the inner-self is telling us. This alone time is your time to plan your journey, reach goals and aspirations, make life-changing decisions (add to your Sunshine in a Bottle or discard into your Pickle Jar). You need this time to bond with you!

"Pickle Jar" the teardrops on your collar, sorrow on your sleeve, betrayal on your buttons, pain on your tie, victim on your brooch-pin, sadness in your trousers, heartache on your jacket – this outfit doesn't *suit* you. You don't wear it well. Get out your LBD "Little Black Dress" and best sparkly shoes, put your lip-gloss on. You're going on a date with the most unique, quirky, topsy-turvy, beautiful, human being – that is you. A little word of warning! You will fall in and out of love, have endless, meaningless arguments, have mood swings, shout, scream, get engaged, say "I do" and get divorced. But! This "emotional rollercoaster" is one hell of a ride. You won't want this relationship to end. If you're up for it! Sign the commitment contract on the following page. Then, get excited…

It is going to be one bumpy, crazy adventure!

MORNING JOTTINGS &
JULIET DATE COMMITMENT

I _____ understand that I am undertaking an intensive, guided encounter with my own inner-self. I commit myself to the twelve-week duration of journaling tasks.

I _____ am willing to commit to daily Morning Jottings pages and weekly Juliet Dates, also the fulfilment of my prompts and tasks.

I _____ further understand that this course will raise issues and emotions for me to deal with.

I _____ commit myself to excellent daily self-care, diet, mantra, meditation, affirmation (if wishing to do so), adequate sleep, exercise and pampering – for the duration of my journaling experience.

Be The Human Sunshine Future You Journey Journal, I _____ come before you just as I am. I am ready to commit to my life story. I am ready to commit to completing my daily Morning Jottings pages, Juliet Dates and journaling practice in separate notebooks to align with the intentions of this journ-book. I will let everyday life inspire my writings and journal prompts.

I _____ commit to creating, speaking, visualising my mantra/s aloud morning, mid-day and evening, at the same time writing it/them on cards or reminders and putting them everywhere that my eye's attention falls – on the fridge, wall, mirror, gadgets and gismos and so on. My mantra/s will be emblazoned in my mind, just as speaking it/them aloud cements firmly in my mind. I visualise my success, I believe it. It has happened.

Signature: _____

Date: _____

My daily mantra will be:

I am the architect of my life.
I build on its foundation.
My efforts are being supported by the
universe, my dreams manifest into
reality right before my eyes.

JOURNAL DATE GUIDELINES

*S*imply follow the simple steps below for your Juliet Date – Reflective Journaling Exercise Experience:

Book two hours into your schedule, call it "Juliet Journal Date – A time to reflect" (book this activity in and it is more likely to happen), calendar this appointment onto all of your gadgets and gismos, everywhere that will prompt/remind you that you have a date. Don't forget you have to prepare, pamper and prune yourself before the date. You have to look your best! I have also created a beautiful mantra for you (no it's not hocus-pocus, but it is a little bit special). I have sprinkled this journ-book with a little "fairy dust" for you. Well! You're never too old to believe in magic are you? Don't worry! I'm not away with the fairies either, I just fly with them sometimes. After all, we all like a bit of adventure don't we… I will talk about the mantra a little later on in the book.

Prepare for this self-care/self-reflection date by deciding where you will take it (the beach, a cafe, under a tree or in a quiet room – your choice) and get your supplies ready.

You will need your journal, separate notebook and writing tools, of course you can take your wand with you – if you must. But! Be sure to hide it in your bag "wink, wink". You might also want to take some water (or a glass of wine or champagne, why not!) to drink and some nibbles – if you're staying at home tell your family you are having "a little me-time, do not disturb". You're ready, the time has come. Have you got butterflies yet? If not, you will have…

Begin by connecting with your breath, simply notice your breath as it enters and leaves your body giving you life. Take four deep breaths in and out, inhale for a count of four, pause, and exhale slowly for a count of four. Repeat this rhythmic breathing four times. This helps you to arrive fully to the moment and to relax. You are much more able to access your intuition (inner wisdom) when in a relaxed state.

For your journaling exercise, write the following two writing prompts at the top of the page:

What I need for my own sense of well-being, replenishment, stress release and/or inner peace at this time is…

My future is an ideal projection of what I envision now…

Pause… and simply listen to what guidance you are receiving from within and from spirit (universal energy source). Start writing and simply capture what you are hearing from within.

Keep your pen moving for at least fifteen minutes – just keep listening within (listen to your wise owl, what is it "twit-twelling" you?) and writing. Don't worry about grammar or making high art. You're writing for yourself, writing to hear your own thinking, your own knowing, and to connect with your own authentic needs. Simply keep your pen moving and trust the process. Trust yourself.

Next…

Read over what you've just written and now write for a further five minutes using this writing prompt to guide you: What is clear to me now is…

Choose one action you would like to take based on the insights you gained from your reflective journaling exercise. Give yourself permission to be spontaneous!

I want you to complete this exercise every week for twelve weeks. Then, reflect back on your date pages and reflect how far you have come. You will be surprised. Surprised at how much you love dating – yourself. You won't want this beautiful relationship to end.

WHAT ARE JOURNAL PROMPTS?

*J*ournal prompts are topics or questions that kick-start your creativity, questions or topics in which you start jotting down your ideas, responses or answers.

The prompt could be a single word, a short phrase, a complete paragraph or even a picture, with the idea being to give you something to focus upon as you write. You can stick very closely to the original prompt or you may wander off at a tangent. You may just come up with rough, disjointed notes or you may end up with something more polished and complete, a scene or even a complete story. The point is to simply start writing without being held back by any inhibitions or doubts.

Sometimes it's hard to start writing when faced with a blank page. Focusing on an unrelated prompt for a while helps get the creative juices flowing. If you write for just ten minutes on a prompt, you should then find it easier to return to the piece you intended to write. You may also find that if you stop trying to think so hard about what you wanted to write and switch your attention to the prompt instead, the words and ideas for your original piece start to come to you after all.

The things you write in response to a prompt may also end up as worthwhile material in their own right. The prompt may give you ideas from which a complete story grows or you may get fresh ideas for another piece you are already working on. It's often surprising how much material you come up with once you start. Writing to a prompt regularly helps to get you into the habit of writing. This can act as a sort of exercise regime, helping to build up your "hand muscles" so that you start to find it easier and easier to write for longer and longer.

Prompts can be a great way to get involved in a writing community. Sometimes writing groups offer a prompt for everyone to write about, with the intention being for everyone to come up with something they can then share. This can be a source of great encouragement, although knowing that others will read what you have written can also inhibit your creativity.

"Simply start writing without being held back by any inhibitions..."

EXAMPLES OF WRITING PROMPTS

*T*he following are basic examples of writing prompts that you could use to spark your imagination. If you want to use one, don't worry about where the ideas take you or whether what you've written is "good". The point is just to get into the flow of writing. You can come back later and polish if you wish to. Dig deep and get creative.

These hips… for instance: these hips have birthed two children, they are meant to unhinge, unlock, get bigger, expand and fit into nothing. I have gotten "jiggy" with these hips to the sound of music within my soul.

These feet… have walked a million miles, have danced and have run. Have stepped in pain, tread in sorrow and run for hope and joy.

Journal Task:

You try it. Use any word you like to ignite your creative spark or use some of these to get you started:

Just passing through…

Life is in the details…

Where it began…

The unseen beauty of it all…

In the distance…

A beautiful disaster…

Without saying a word…

Here comes the day…

WHEN SHOULD I JOURNAL?

*Y*our journaling will be most effective if you do it daily for about twenty minutes (ideally half an hour). It is good to set aside a certain time for journaling, whether it be morning or evening (if you have decided not to commit to the morning pages just yet) whichever you prefer; find a quiet space where you won't be distracted. Begin anywhere you feel comfortable, and forget spelling and punctuation. Privacy is key if you are to write without censor. Write quickly, as this frees your brain from "should" and other blocks to successful journaling. If it helps, pick a theme for the day, week or month, you can use a separate notebook to complete this exercise. For example, some themes you could pick would be: the beach, going global, the anger within etc. The most important rule of all is — there are no rules.

Through your writing you'll discover that your journal is an all-accepting, non-judgmental friend. And he/she (if you name your journal) may provide the cheapest therapy you will ever get. Maybe, when journaling, add some light blue scented candles for healing to your space, and listen to some inspirational music creating all around ambience. Write down your thoughts, feelings and ideas. Even if only a word, few short phrases or sentences. Do it! These inspirational moments may fade sooner than you realise.

If you get stuck for ideas and have nothing concrete to write about, try recording snippets of: conversations you overhear, facts, feelings, fantasies, descriptions, quotes, poems, images, paintings, songs, nature, people, animals or anything you feel may have inspired you. Create pictures to illustrate your words, externalising your thoughts and feelings invariably leads to a sunnier, positive you.

MORNING JOURNALING

"OPEN AS IF THE PETAL, THE FLOWER, AMONG THE PROFUSION, FREE-FALL INTO THE PLACE WHERE EVERYTHING IS MUSIC. APPRECIATE THE BREATH."

SUNSHINE SCROLLS

*M*ost of us never get time entirely for ourselves. Even in the alone time we spend most of it worrying about others, caring for our family and loved ones or listening to friends. It's very important to set aside space for yourself each day, even if only twenty minutes (ideally half an hour) devoted entirely to yourself. Find a place inside or outside; a space you can sit quietly and catch your breath before beginning the day. Most of you may feel this is a selfish thing to do – yes it is. You need this time to recharge your batteries, revitalise and invigorate yourself – mornings are a great time to do this and to journal.

During your early-morning journaling, allow a place within to open and let parts of yourself release into your jottings that you didn't know were holding on. Feel all of the hard places within your heart and body yield to a great softness carried on your breath, and be filled with compassion for the parts of you that are always doing, trying, anticipating, making or breaking. Allow your mind to be still. Grow into the moment. Simply follow your breath and let the moments stretch. Feel a great faith wash over you, a knowing, all that needs to be done will get done. Don't worry – there is enough, enough time and energy for all that is needed. Appreciate the breath.

This life reality us humans live: always aspiring to be our best, to be more than what is. Longing for and sometimes finding meaning and connection with ourselves and that which is larger than ourselves, we are undone; undone in trying to make sense and meaning of it all. Allow a great tenderness for yourself and the world to open up inside, know that you belong to this time, to this space, to each other, to the world and to something that is both within and larger than it all. Let it hold and sustain you as your words fall from experiences, emotions, mind – to page.

You can use your morning journaling time to write the Morning Jottings & Scrolls. But, if you would like to practice journaling first, create your Morning Jottings pages later on. Set a date when you will begin your Morning Jottings and stick to it.

Journal Task:

Set a date to sign your committment contract (you can come back to this page when ready to sign, if you're not willing to commit just yet).

Choose which writing tool you will use to sign the contract (your favorite pen) and when you're ready to commit (take your time to decide, you must take this commitment seriously) savour the seconds when you sign the contract – you are now a *Be the Human Sunshine* Journal Keeper.

You're on a secret mission to change your life.

EVENING JOURNALING

"IT IS WHEN WE LOOK OUT TO THE NIGHT SKIES
WE COME TO UNDERSTAND WE ARE PART OF THE
BIGGER PLANS, AND A LITTLE MORE THAN THE
SPACE IN-BETWEEN."

SUNSHINE SCROLLS

*I*f you decide to journal in the evening, it is really nice to
set the scene with some beautiful calming music. Choose
music that has flowing melodies rather than fragmented and
disjointed chords. Select low pitch and slow tempo music, try
using sounds from nature such as ocean waves or tranquil
birdsong. Classical music is also highly effective.

Prior to writing in your journal: sit down, preferably for a
few quiet moments, in a still, dark and quiet area indoors
or outdoors and observe the heavens. The vastness and
infinite space is quite awesome: to infinity and beyond.

Journal Prompt:

What does the night-time mean to you? What does it
represent? What is your inner-self saying to you about this
infinite space?

JOURN-MAP

*B*efore setting off on your journaling voyage – you've got to have a plan. A plan is a map of intent, a guide, a route, a path, a direction, a plan of action. A plan isn't a dream – it's something you intend on doing rather than something you want to do. A plan gives your life structure and purpose. It's a place to map your intentions for this journey. What do you want to achieve from this experience, from your life? What are your dreams? To what destinations do your dreams take you?

I understand, not all plans work out all of the time, but if you have one it helps – it keeps you in control of where you're going, or at least hoping to get to. Every captain needs a map, a compass, a route to follow. If you don't have a plan you lose course – get lost in unknown waters and get hijacked by the "Life-surprise Pirates" and there is nothing worse than being caught off-guard. At least if you have a plan then you don't go through life surprised by what happens, instead you're a little prepared.

As you know the life-weather can hit us hard – thunderstorms will come, circumstances and commitments will change, things that are beyond our control. Have no fear! The plan means you're ready: you have your umbrella, raincoat and wellington boots on. The plan can be reviewed and changed at any time. If you don't plan, your dreams will remain just that, a dream.

Work out a rough guide of what it is you would like to achieve in your life – set goals and basic deadlines. Figure out all of the necessary steps it takes to achieve your goals, list them then begin. Work out what it is you want to do with your life and plan it, work out all of the logical steps you need to take to reach your goals and achieve your dreams.

Journal Prompt:

Create a plan of intent. Work out a rough guide of what it is you would like to achieve in your life – set goals and basic deadlines. Get excited! Plan it like a life-party!

MORNING JOTTINGS &
JULIET DATE CHECK IN

*A*s I stated earlier, I would be asking you how you are getting on with your Morning Jottings and Juliet Date. I know it will take time to adjust your day/week to these regular journaling practices, but if you stick to using them you will notice over time just how much you enjoy spending time with yourself.

You must at least give them a try – three months at least. Just three months to write seven hundred and fifty words every morning, set your alarm clock half an hour/an hour earlier and allow for the many times you will hit the "snooze button" for five more minutes. If you write on your computer/laptop your word count will be listed. I promise you, after three months you will write a further three months and so on… Who knows it may lead you on the "write path" to your personal enlightenment. By the end of your jottings you will be ready for the day, brain drained of negativity and ready for a positive day ahead.

As with the Morning Jottings, your Juliet Date is as equally important, this is your time to again spend with yourself, a date with you. As with anything in life, if you want both the jottings and date to work you must make the effort. The universe will not give you the moon and the stars if you only reach for the rooftops… nothing in life comes easy, it takes work, dedication and commitment.

Journal Prompts:

What does it feel like writing my Morning Jottings & Juliet Date? What is this experience teaching me? What am I learning about myself? Can I feel the change within? Am I moving forward, or am I stuck?

If you're stuck keep going, just think of all the hurdles you have overcome in life, you get over them in the end. Don't quit! But of course, if you have given them a lengthy try with fullest commitment and they're not working for you and you're not a morning person, stick with the Juliet Date or vise versa.

Check in twelve-weekly with your jottings and weekly with your date and document in your separate notebook how you're getting on, describe your feelings at length. You can, if you wish, discuss your Juliet Date in your Morning Jottings, this is the perfect place to write to yourself about your date. I shall leave this up to you, but you must check in; check in keeps you on track. No getting hijacked by the "Life-surprise Pirates" they eagerly await to jump aboard your "time" ship. Remember! You're the captain; you are in charge.

What is your

Mission Statement?

*W*hat is your mission statement? What is it you dedicate your life to? Relax! There are no right or wrong answers here; it's a personal choice. Maybe, you don't already have an answer, this may be your reason for journaling, and it is my hope that you will by the end of this book – or at least have an idea.

You're probably thinking "What is your mission statement?" My own life has been driven by a few things over the years, and I would say this piece is the perfect place to tell you where the inspiration for the name of my journal collection came from: it was given as an intended mission statement for myself and others to hopefully arrive at or be touched by at some point in my/our lives. Although every person's journey will take them on different paths, eventually everybody will… (I have saved this piece for you at the end of the book, don't look just yet. Not even a sneaky peek) have patience.

What has driven me? I am not intending to push my religion on anybody here I am simply stating my reasons for the drive in my life. At the age of eighteen I had a calling from God to be a nun, a calling that has lived with me every day of my life since then. I won't go into heavy detailed reasons for me not entering the convent or the spiritual experiences I have had the privilege of since then – other than; my mother asked me to seriously think about it and live a little before deciding. So I did. And, you guessed it! I didn't enter. Do I regret it? No. I made time for my regret and let it inspire a mission statement I would try to use throughout my life: to always "*Be the Human Sunshine*".

I often struggled against my calling and made lots of mistakes along the way, but there remained an ache within my soul, the deepest part of my inner-self, to follow my calling in one way or another. The calling had triggered something unexplainable but understandable to other nuns and those called to God (the light, goodness, direction) etc. It got me thinking. I am being called to God or something that can only be explained as a light that "illuminates my life and path every day". So, if I didn't go then how can I go now? How do I go about improving my life and the lives of others in a way that would align with my teenage calling, now not as a nun but as a mother, wife, daughter, sister, friend, colleague and human being. My conclusion; I have always used the calling as my conscience, to be as decent a person as I can be, to tread through life causing as little damage (hurt or pain) as possible, to treat others with kindness, compassion, respect and dignity. It is something I have dedicated my life to and has become my personal mission statement.

My calling was hard to live by at times (remember! I am only human) as it's not so easy to be sunshine all of the time. I have had grey days, fought thunderstorms and raging torrents lots of times, but the voice and light within became my spiritual compass – my lamp. I trust it. I may get lost but I always find my way again. Although I did not accept my calling at eighteen; I have for the last twenty-three years, through my work, dedicated my life to people from England and all around the world: those affected by illness, addiction, disadvantage, domestic violence, social exclusion, mental illness, oppression and a variety of other causes contributing to homelessness. So I believe in one way or another I have accepted my calling. This was the way it was meant to be. It's something I hope one day I will be able to do on a grander scale in other parts of the world. And, I guess "*Being the Human Sunshine*" isn't such a bad *habit* to get into… is it!

Journal Prompt:

What is your mission statement?

WHO AM I?
WHAT IS MY LIFE PURPOSE?

*M*any of us have asked ourselves this question many times; "Who am I? What is my life purpose?" My understanding of these questions is: we are all instruments through which the Divine Creator manifests in this world; we are here to radiate human sunshine; the loving-kindness, harmony, serenity and beauty of the Divine Creator.

It is our purpose, our task as human beings to freely and joyfully radiate love, harmony and beauty into this world. When we abide in that reality, rather than our own, we find that we are ambassadors of the Divine, sent on a glorious mission to deliver human sunshine, beauty, wonder and joy.

Every human being and living thing will die, that is fact, yet we are all given a measure of free will to choose how to live the days that we are blessed with. There is no higher calling than to honour and glorify our Creator by living an unselfish life filled with love, compassion and joy for ourselves, each other and the world. Therefore! You are faced with the choice and probably one of the hardest choices you will ever have to make, and you will have to live with the consequences of those choices: "Are you on the side of the Angels or Demons?"

Journal Prompt:

If all the karma you have earned in your life so far came back around to you today, do you think it would be good or bad?

If good, how would you like to be rewarded? If bad, how do you think you could improve it from today onwards? How will you live your remaining days? Will you live your remaining days with un-forgiveness, selfishness, regret or anger or will you choose a path of love, harmony and beauty?

"It is our task as human beings to joyfully radiate love..."

"BE THE PHENOMENAL,
BEAUTIFUL, UNIQUE PERSON
THAT IS YOU
– GO FORTH ON YOUR LIFE
JOURNEY, SHARE YOUR
INNER SUNBEAM & DELIVER
HUMAN SUNSHINE."

*E*very person is a phenomenal, beautiful, unique creation of the Divine Creator:

Every human being is an on-going work-in-progress, with miraculous potential for positive change and transformation. Every moment, the privilege of life offers a new opportunity to express Divine beauty in your presence.

It is the greatest joy in life to think and act with beauty:

In every moment there is a sunbeam that longs to be radiated through you. When you each allow Divine beauty to freely manifest through your thoughts, words and deeds, then you align with the Divine and begin to fulfil your greatest purpose – our Divine purpose.

What does it mean to be beautiful?

To be beautiful is to let your thoughts, words and deeds deliver human sunshine into the world: to share the sun of the heart, your inner-sunbeam with everyone that you meet on your life journey. To greet and treat each and every human being with compassion, respect, dignity, forgiveness, kindness, grace, love and joy. To be beautiful, is to express joyful gratitude for all that you have and will receive in the privilege of life. To be beautiful is to see the ever-present Divine beauty that is everywhere, in everyone and everything.

Let the beauty of life be the only beauty that illuminates your path – that is enduring beauty. Facial and physical beauty comes and goes, but the beauty that shines from a loving human sunshine heart, lasts a whole lifetime. Seeing real beauty is not to limit your vision with sight, but to feel it in the deepest parts of yourself and in the sunbeam of others. Simply be beautiful.

Perhaps this seems all too easy: "simply be beautiful". But! To be human sunshine can be quite challenging and liberating as well as immensely satisfying. You will notice over time how your ideals and understanding of beauty changes, urging you to share even greater expressions of beauty into the world through your own fragrant thoughts, deeds and words, free-fall into the beauty of today. Today is

59

a new day, let today's beauty radiate in all of its fullness, in all of its warmth, in all of its capacity – through the sunshine that is you.

Journal Prompt:

"I am awesome because" or "I am wonderful because…" Now write a list dedicated to the awesomeness of you: all of your achievements, successes, talents, skills, quirky interests, qualifications, best experiences and proudest moments. Big and small in no particular order, just write them down. Going right back to when you were a child.

I then want you to write a letter to yourself in twelve weeks' time, "Dear awesome, wonderful me". Put this letter away… and read it again in twelve months' time. Then, repeat this process every year, thereafter. If you continue with your journaling experience, through your "awesome, wonderful you" lists and letters, you will notice how much you have grown and moved forward in your life. Don't worry about set-backs. Set-backs are lessons. This is the school of life. You are forever the student. How beautiful is that! Every day offers new gifts, treasures and life-lessons… now that is nearly as awesome and cool as you!

I COME BEFORE
YOU JUST AS I AM!

*W*hen we resist acceptance, it's called suffering. But when we can completely let go and not struggle against it, when we can embrace the groundlessness of our situation and relax into its dynamic quality, that's called enlightenment. If you come to accept what's done is done, you are left with *you* just as you are. Accepting really is easy – because it is exactly what it says on the tin – accepting. You don't have to change, improve or strive for perfection or the expectation of others, "simply accept". Accept yourself with all the emotional bruises, scars, brokenness, weaknesses, longing, sorrows and pain. It doesn't mean we have to be happy with absolutely everything about ourselves or our lives, we are simply going to accept all that we are – right now, be grateful and grow from it.

It takes a lot of courage and guts to accept you can't change anything. You can't go back to a past moment and change it; this moment is all you have. People make mistakes. Sometimes they're small, big or very serious ones that cause us distress or severe emotional pain but more often than not the mistakes aren't meant to be deliberate or personal. They just happen. It wasn't necessarily because the person intended to be cruel or unkind, but because they were naive and foolish. Some people don't know any better; maybe it was the way they were brought up, learned behaviour? And for others, some people jump the fence thinking the grass is greener on the other side. People trip into the "mistake mud" once in a while and will fall face-first again and again. "Why?" They are human; nobody's perfect, no-one. We are all the same, all the same. Breathing, beating, human beings and we all mess up now and then.

In accepting what is done is done, we let go, we release feelings of anger, resentment, revenge and regret. You can accept you are a courageous, phenomenal human being because of all of the hurts and things that have happened to you, not in spite of them. To get the most from your life you have to embrace all of the hurtful, painful experiences as being a part of you and sit with them without trying to fade them or fix them. Pain demands to be felt. Let your experiences shape your future, to be a positive force to such extent that you couldn't imagine your life without them; they are what make you, you. Don't wish to change a thing. Just accept. Then – move on.

I know we can do this, because I have experienced and have seen in others the ability to go into and embrace the places of darkness, despair, sorrow, pain and longing. And through all of these experiences I have found great courage and faith in the human spirit. These experiences have shaped who I am. I hold a great tenderness for the courage of us humans, we fall and rise again and again, expanding to hold all that is true, accepting what we cannot change even though at times it seems impossible, unbearable and out of reach.

We hang onto the branches, too afraid to dig deep into the roots, reject forgiveness, hold back from accepting for fear of the longing – we're only human. It is during these times we can lean in and on to that something that is both within and larger than it all; faith, faith not only in the mystery, but also in ourselves.

I am guided by the path that illuminates, by an ache to take the necessary risk to accept, to live close to what is within and around me, and "yes" I'm sometimes afraid. Afraid all will become too much and I will suffocate in the expectancy to accept. In these moments my soul is compelled by a deep hunger that goes further than the roots and it urges me forward to live this privilege to its fullest. I let go of the things I cannot change; I let go of the branches and free-fall into the place where everything is music – into the place of exquisite beauty and gut-wrenching sorrow of being fully alive. Therefore, I know we can do this, we can do it together. Don't lose out on the only time you have to forgive, to heal, to love, to live, to be human. Accept all that is done is done, let go, choose to forgive and get on with your life. Things will improve enormously. Yesterday has gone, tomorrow has not yet come, we have only this moment. Accept life. Appreciate the breath.

ACCEPT EACH OTHER

"NO ONE IS BORN HATING ANOTHER PERSON BECAUSE OF THE COLOUR OF HIS SKIN, OR HIS BACKGROUND, OR HIS RELIGION. PEOPLE MUST LEARN TO HATE, AND IF THEY CAN LEARN TO HATE, THEY CAN BE TAUGHT TO LOVE, FOR LOVE COMES MORE NATURALLY TO THE HUMAN HEART THAN ITS OPPOSITE."

LONG WALK TO FREEDOM
THE AUTOBIOGRAPHY OF NELSON MANDELA

We are all the same breathing, beating human beings, yet we are all different. It is that simple… each and every one of us are both the same and different. I know it sounds strange, but it's true. We have always been different, we will always be different. We must learn to accept our differences with patience, tolerance, understanding and love or else we will be in trouble forever.

The first step in finding any peace, on either an individual or social basis, is the loving acceptance of "what is". Our diversity must be accepted, not denied or attacked. There can never be peace without acceptance of "what is". All war, all human conflict is our resistance to the way things actually are. We continually fight against "what is", and the battle continually fails. Our diversity is the very reason that we exist. We exist to be individuals, we exist to be different. We must accept this simple fact if we want to find the heart of peace. We must simply accept "what is". Diversity is only conquered with tolerance, understanding, patience and loving kindness. In accepting "what is" we move freely together, allowing the music of life to move us beyond one song, prejudice, expectation or limitation. Understand that the first beat of change leads to the second, third and so on.

The challenge is not about changing the world outside of us, the challenge is about changing the world within us. To see a new world, we must see with new eyes "through the window that is the heart". You change; and the world can change with you. Firstly, you must open your heart to speak a new language, one that cultivates love and compassion. Changes do happen from the open hearted "infectious" it gives us hope for a new world. Suddenly! What once did not grow amongst the mountains and rocks is the beauty of a thousand fields. When broken, we become the rock, crumbled and shattered, we reach out in prayer often struggling to open the door between ourselves and the Divine mystery. The door is a mere illusion. When we send a message of prayer to the Divine he is reaching out his message to us. And in all of our attempts to reach him, he is actually attempting to reach us. So, when you think he is not listening or you are feeling separated from him when searching for him on the outside, search inside yourself. For what you seek among the branches and trees, only appears in the roots.

Journal Prayer Prompt:

As we embrace the music of life let us dance, dancing into the unafraid, unafraid to be vulnerable to ourselves, to each other and to the world. To be friends no matter our cultural beliefs, religion, faith, ethnicity, gender, colour or world view. Let us comfort without questioning, allowing moments of complete silence, real grace and simple understanding, to be human in times of distress.

Hold a willingness to transform the pain and suffering in others, transforming the pain and suffering within ourselves. "Divine mystery, hold us". Hold us together, one by one, skin to skin as we open our hearts to the diversity of others embracing their differences and our own – for we are all unique expressions contributing fragrance to the world. Hold us as we accept. Accept ourselves, and each other. Opening our eyes to see through only one thing – through the window that is the heart.

"ALL ANSWERS WILL BE
GIVEN IN TIME AND IN THE
KNOWING HAVING FAITH IS
JUST ENOUGH."

*W*e are a right bunch of complex human beings living in a complex world. It's as if our life is one big maze through which the "What is the meaning of life-solver" must find a route. Although the through-route has twists and turns and is not designed to be as difficult to navigate – we still get lost. Life is like this most of the time. We are full of questions and awaiting answers at our every turn: why are we here? What is our purpose? What religion/faith, belief/ cultural system or route shall I follow? Why aren't all religions uniting and not fighting, surely this is not the message of those we have faith and belief in. Why do awful things happen to people? Why do people behave the way they do toward other people (hurting, killing)? Why are there wars? Why do children and people suffer and die? Why are people hungry? Why are people homeless? Where do we go when we die? Some of it we can piece together ourselves but some of it we will never know. It is quite fascinating isn't it! All of these whooshing thoughts are like vertigo, they make us dizzy trying to work out the answers. Some things I am afraid will always remain beyond our comprehension. That's the way it's meant to be. Things will go unexpectedly wrong, people will act in ways that we don't understand or "cannot comprehend" and things will often not make sense.

One evening while journaling I was asking myself some of the above questions while looking out to the night skies and out into the universe, then a sunshine scroll came to me: "It is when we look out to the night skies we come to understand we are part of the bigger plans a little more than the space in-between". Then, I simply let go of the need for answers that for now would remain unanswered.

And, it makes sense: we are little people in a big universe and part of something we question every day. We won't get the answers we seek beyond just yet, but in time. It's as if our lives are caught up in the maze puzzle called "Answer Seekers". We are always curious, questioning, wondering, seeking, trying, problem solving, deciphering – trying to find the right path, we get lost in the quest for the meaning of life and we forget to appreciate the breath. We forget to live in the moment, and in all of our seeking all we get access to is another part of the maze.

"We are always curious, questioning, wondering, seeking, trying…"

"Do not journey through life like a dog searching for invisible bones..."

It's all complicated and strange sometimes isn't it! We'll never be able to understand everything, all we end up with is assumptions and no concrete answers. That's what life is, the maze puzzle. The mystery. If you just let go and accept that there will always be lots of unanswered questions, you release all of the stresses and worries that prevent you from living right now. You create a purpose for your reasons to be here, rather than waiting for a purpose. It's as simple as that. A little *Be the Human Sunshine* statement I live by that frees my mind from some of the never-ending questions and assumptions is: "All answers will be given in time and in the knowing having faith is just enough". That is enough for me.

Try it.

"EVERYWHERE YOU ARE
LOOKING, OR SEEKING,
SEE THROUGH ONLY ONE
THING, THROUGH THE
WINDOW THAT IS
THE HEART."

*E*verywhere you look, there are countless people seeking, searching and hoping for some hidden secret that will lead to happiness. Thousands of self-help and spiritual guidance books have been written, yet too many people still wander endlessly unaware, unhappy and lacking insight into their own unique purpose. Yet the answer is simple. To feel your own existence is to understand how fragile life is, life is a privilege, a gift. To embrace the presence that is the mystery in your heart; through goodness, kindness, compassion and forgiveness is to understand what beauty really is.

To see through the window that is the heart, is what sight truly is. The greatest secret of life happiness is... to be a lamp for others where there is darkness. What cries out for healing is not always physical pain, such as illness, it is also emotional pain. We as humans often plod into the darkness, hiding in: depression, despair, hurt feelings, longing, sadness, disappointment, anxiety, sorrow and bereavement.

Helping heal the pain we see around us and within us is a part of how we light our lamp – the sunbeam. Other human beings await the healing touch of the Divine that comes about through us. In faith we are freed from the darkness. This freedom allows us to journey more confidently to touch the heart of the mystery – real beauty is not found in the face but found in the heart, also the soul, and is produced within ourselves.

Some wander through life looking for diamonds when all the while the rarest jewel beats inside your chest.

Journal Prompt:

How will you open your heart to others today?

Sunshine Scrolls

The Fear

"HOLD ME" AS I REACH INTO MY INTERIOR
CANVAS, ONE I WISH TO PAINT EXTERIORLY BUT
SOMETIMES FEAR. FOR FEAR OFTEN HOLDS ME
TO THE BOUNDARIES OF MY LIMITLESS MIND,
AND THERE ARE TIMES WHEN I DARE TO NOT TO
LIVE, BUT MERELY SURVIVE. IN THESE MOMENTS
US HUMANS CALL TIME. "HOLD ME".

SUNSHINE SCROLLS

There is only one thing that makes our dreams impossible for us to achieve, the fear of failure. Fear is part of being alive. It is a natural response to the anticipation of pain and comes from the realisation that if we live and love fully, we will feel the losses that are inevitably part of the constant cycle of change. Becoming fearless isn't the point. That's impossible. While many workshops/seminars offer us the promise to eliminate all fear in our lives forever, and what we may experience throughout the workshop/seminar is the illusion of fear, but not real fear. How can this be true?

Sometimes, when in a dangerous situation, fear can be life-preserving. It is also a natural reaction to moving closer to the truth. We gain strength, courage and confidence by every hard blow or experience in which we really stop to look fear in the face. We are able to say to ourselves "although I feared this decision, change, interview, betrayal or loss etc. I can take the next thing that comes along". You must do the things those fear thoughts say you cannot do. The most important lesson is learning how to control fear, and how to be free from it. Fearless is not the absence of fear, it's not being completely unafraid, fearless is having fear, having doubts, lots of them. Forget safety; be fearless and live where you fear to live, living in spite of those things that scare you to death. Be notorious, take a risk, risk it for the freedom, to see what is true, to find what it is you really want in the deepest parts of yourself. Risk it all; for the adventure of being alive. You get to make the choices in your life, and you will live with the consequences of those choices. But if you want to live a life close to your deepest desires and dreams, you have to risk knowing who it is that you really are. To dream or desire allows us freedom, and while there are many children that fear the dark; the real tragedy of life is when as adults we fear the light. There is no life in that. Now you know this, you can choose.

Be fearless of falling madly in love again even though you have been hurt before, as I said, fear is moving closer to the truth, and sometimes the truth is what we don't want to hear, what we fear most. When things are shaky and nothing is working, realise that you just may well be on the verge of something. You may well realise that fear of really living is a very vulnerable place, and that tenderness for yourself can go either way. You can either shut down and feel resentful for not making the change or you can touch in on that throbbing quality and make even the tiniest of change seem significant. It's a start.

"Be fearless of falling madly
in love..."

"When our heart is full of sorrow and pain, so much so, we feel we can't hold it all. Remember how small our eyes are, yet they hold the world."

Rejoicing in the ordinary things or the simple life is not sentimental, it takes guts and courage. Letting go is fearless. Then moving on and knowing it's going to be okay is fearless too, you just have to believe in yourself. Each time we drop our complaints and our fears allowing every day good fortune, like just living, inspire us; we enter into fearless territory and into a warrior's world.

Journal Prompt:

Tell me what you ache for? What do you fear most? And, would you risk it all for the adventure of being fully alive?

The Sorrow

"ALL THE WHILE THE HEART SLEEPS, SILENTLY
BEATING, UNTIL AWOKEN BY THE BANG OF
THE LIFE DRUM. EVERY HARSH BLOW PIERCES
THE HEART AWAKENING OUR SOUL."

SUNSHINE SCROLLS

" Every hard blow we receive in life pierces the heart..."

*E*very living human being has a time of awakening. Sometimes it is gradual and sometimes it is sudden and instant. To some, it may come in a fleeting moment by a hard harsh blow, a disappointment, a betrayal, loss, bereavement or because the heart has been broken through something that happens suddenly. At the time it seems cruel, uninvited and unforgiving but, without consciously realising, at the same time this sorrow guest is a blessing – a life lesson. Our outlook changes, insight deepens, independence and freedom is felt in our intimacy, compassion is shown toward ourselves, also in our attitude towards others. A person who is unwilling to forgive forever remains in constant constraint and unable to move forward into life. A soul that is awoken by all that has broken us or instilled fear becomes, in one fleeting moment, a different person. Sorrow is the bringer of joy and every hard blow we receive in life pierces the heart and awakens our feelings to sympathise with others, and every comfort (mine; be it faith or hope) lulls us to sleep. When we reach out, lean in, and on – letting go of the sorrow, we become aware of the mystery. We hold onto faith and live in hope that during these sorrowful times "we are held". As a student it is really important to remember, you may need to revise in the future! The cure for your pain is the pain itself. You only truly heal when you have opened and touched the pain that hurts you deep within, the pain that blesses and heals you. The darkness is your candle, the pain your messengers, listen to them and answer them.

When broken, we become the rock, crumbled and shattered, we reach out in prayer often struggling to open the door between ourselves and the Divine mystery. The door is a mere illusion. When we send a message of prayer to the Divine he is reaching out his message to us. And in all of our attempts to reach him, he is actually attempting to reach us. So, when you think he is not listening to you (understand you are in a queue) or are feeling separated from him searching him on the outside, search inside yourself. For what you search among the branches, only appears in the roots.

⋆ Have Faith All Will Be Held:

When we touch the very depths of our own sorrow, when we sit with our pain without trying to fix it, staying present with our experience, the feeling, we are awoken. We connect with our awakened heart, open and wounded. Don't reject the feeling, don't pull away; hold it, embrace it, let it soften you, be unafraid to be vulnerable to yourselves, each other and the world. Have faith, let go, lean in and on. You are held by something larger than it all. It holds us; as we hold on. The mystery.

Journal Task:

Repeat this affirmation for a few moments when feeling the weight of your troubles: "Though my feelings besiege me and often I stumble and fall, my heart will not fear. The Divine is my strength and shield. I am held."

What is it your pain is telling you?

Longing:
The Butterfly Effect

"How does one become a butterfly?" The answer is this simple: "you must want to learn to fly so much that you are willing to give up being a caterpillar". There have been times when I have seen a beautiful butterfly flying freely, I am reminded to pause and enjoy the miracle of their life, change and flight. We all seek our wings and that "something" we cannot define, "a longing for freedom and freedom from the longing". Our soul butterfly compels us to remove the fear from what we long for or do not know, encouraging us to continue in the search to find out who we really are or forever we remain the caterpillar.

As humans we often evade the longing and desire to live fully, in many cases this evading and fear leads to emotional numbness (numbing out) hidden behind the veil of alcohol, drugs, overwork etc. Often, in many cases, a person's longing to find out who they really are can be stunted by others. And it is during these times we need to ask ourselves some questions. "Should I risk all for the longing to see what is true in the deepest part of myself, to betray another as not to betray my own soul. For the freedom to make whatever choices I want to make in my life and to live by the consequences of those choices; but in making them I know I can learn, expand and grow."

These are some of the hard questions we have to ask ourselves sometimes, and for some – they may seem selfish. But if you really look deep within, to see what it is you really long for in your life, you come to understand your development so far may have been shaped by selflessness and your commitment to others, and not yourself. Sometimes you have to be a little selfish.

If you want to live skin to skin with your deepest dreams and desires you have to be willing to risk the person that you think you are at this moment, for the person you can be. Your longing has to be larger than the fear, the desire more fierce than the pain. You must be willing to betray another as not to betray your own soul. *I know you can do this*. I have experienced and seen in others the ability to go into those darkened places of despair, sorrow, pain and longing. And through all of these experiences have found great courage and faith in the human spirit. These experiences have shaped who I am, I am now all I longed for and you may ask "how?" and I will say it simply, "you have to be willing to fly". I hold a great tenderness for the courage of us humans, we fall and rise again and again, expanding to hold all that is true, accepting all we cannot change even though at times it seems impossible, unbearable, out of reach, we still choose life!

We hang onto the branches, too afraid to dig deep into the roots, reject forgiveness, hold back from accepting for fear of the longing – we are only human. It is during these times we can lean in and on to that "something" that is both within and larger than it all: "faith", faith not only in the mystery but in ourselves. The metaphor of the butterfly for transformation is profound: the banal-looking caterpillar becomes the beautiful, radiant butterfly. Before the caterpillar becomes a butterfly it prepares its cocoon as if it were dying. What the caterpillar thinks is the end, is actually the beginning. Caterpillars intuitively know their alignment with nature, when it's time to start spinning their bed to sleep in. You never see another caterpillar wriggling over and saying, "It's caterpillar bed time." It's intuitive. Change is intuitive.

So many people are waiting for someone to tap them on the shoulder or wriggle over to give them permission to reach for their dreams – to break from their restrictive cocoon, to fly.

"Some people are settling down, some people are settling and some people refuse to settle for anything less than butterflies." *Sarah Jessica Parker.*

What are you settling for right now?

Journal Prompt:

Where are you in your life? Are you a butterfly, soaring, enjoying your beautiful manifestation, or are you a caterpillar receiving the intuitive message that it's time for your transition – time for change? Are you sitting around waiting for permission or affirmation of the next step on your journey? Are you looking with longing for change but holding onto fear, too scared to break out of your shell seeing it as "too much hard work" which makes you disinclined to act upon it? Or are you seeing the obstacles as learning experiences, pathways to your own inner strength and mastery, viewing all experiences as the student of life?

Okay! It's time to live fully, to step into the complete new version of you. This means letting go of everything in your life that does not serve you, dispose all into your Pickle Jar. You don't have to do everything at once, simply take it slowly, just like the caterpillar. Take the first step and wriggle out from your comfort zone, in taking this first step, believe me the rest will follow, you will become empowered with every step. You will find that you are supported. It can be a little daunting, scary and painful at first, shedding the "old you". Have no fear, you are held. And I too, am right here with you every step of the way.

When we let go of what is not serving us we make room for what will. And just like the caterpillar out of its "cocoon"

"It's time to live fully, to step into the complete new version of you..."

it's a worthwhile flight. You emerge as the butterfly… you get to fly with your dreams and out into the successes that so far have eluded you. Climb up and out of your cocoon, out of the restrictive environment that has held you back and your dreams will be waiting there for you.

Simply be the beautiful butterfly, *fly freely,* do not look above or below at the scenery of life "be a part of it". Spread your wings and have yourself a little butterfly effect.

Love

"May you both savour each discovery of touch as you infinitely unfold each other, layer upon layer, by body, your story, or simply the moments that pass between you, whether it be for the first time or again, and again. Share with me the tales of your heart; offer them to me in colour, in detail. Let us hold them as if the rainbow – a covenant between you and I. Let the colours of our stories spin out on multi-coloured yarn as they intertwine. But! We won't share all too soon. We will stop weaving and allow room for longing, for some new story to tell during our seamless conversations. Then, in the eloquent silence, let openness be found in our pleasure and our pain, confusion and wisdom, available to us each moment of our ordinary, everyday lives. We will hold on even if those stories take us to the places that frighten or have broken us. We will take lead "as if we were warriors" and as we go forward we will know that our intimacy is a shared, comfortable solitude, a silence born out of real stories – flesh, bone, respect and love."

"When suffering a broken heart we become afraid to open ourselves up to future love for fear of further pain. It is not our task to seek love, but to seek and find all the barriers within ourselves that we have built against it."

When you touch your heart intimately and openly, allowing it also to be touched by others, you discover its capacity, its vastness, its forever – eternity. It has no ending to the possibilities to love. The heart is limitless. In opening your heart you discover the warmth, gentleness, kindness and forgiveness – the sunbeam.

Journal Prompt:

What is the name of your heartbeat in this moment? (Example: my heartbeat is named compassion, empathy, forgiveness, one more heartbeat after another, a gift. My heartbeat is joy, my heartbeat is sunrise, my heartbeat is my children, Romeo… etc.)

What does your heart look/feel like? Draw it. As you draw your heart – write in it all of the names/feelings/hopes that your heart beats for…

Phoenix
That Is You

*M*y goodness… life is difficult. Do we stand in the centre of the fire, or do we shrink back? If we shrink back from all of life's raging flames how do we expect to learn, grow or rise from the ashes. As much as I like sunshine I also love a rainbow; it gives me a sense of hope. I am realistic; if life was all fluffy clouds and sunshine we wouldn't appreciate moments of joy and we wouldn't meet courage or strength (the warrior within) in the embers. In those moments of joy we forget about the fire, what the heat is really like. It's only in the stories of our struggles, of our burning and rising, that we feel the flame.

I know it sounds strange and of course we all need a break from struggle now and again, but be grateful for it some of the time. Struggle is very grounding; it makes you appreciate. Of course there will be other times when the fire will surround us – when we will have to stand in the centre of it – torn open by what is beyond our control whether it be love, betrayal, bereavement, sorrow, pain, longing or despair. But! You must remember the flames that surround us are also the flames that transform us.

When everything seems like an uphill struggle and the next obstacle meets you on your journey – understand. That's what life is. The way it's meant to be; a series of pain, pit-falls, struggles and disappointments. Every person feels emotional pain or struggle in one way or another no matter their wealth, status or circumstance. It's not about the uphill struggle or the mountain climb; it's about the falling also the rising, again and again the "Phoenix that is you".

Journal Prompt:

How many times have you risen like the Phoenix?

Appreciate
the Breath

THE SOFT MORNING BREEZE CARRIES THE
FRAGRANCE OF LIFE UPON ITS BREATH. WE
MUST GET UP AND TAKE THAT IN, THAT IS THE
BREEZE THAT LETS US LIVE. BREATHE BEFORE
IT'S GONE."

SUNSHINE SCROLLS

*S*ometimes we forget the breath, we take it for granted. It moves and expands in and out. And through our anxieties we spend a long time: sighing, suffocating, drowning and feeling disconnected, but those moments of grace come and we feel all of the hard places in our heart and body embrace a softness carried upon it. Our shoulders drop; our minds stop and the small but familiar ache eases and the moments stretch along with the breath. We simply follow it; we take all in deeply and hold it close for a few seconds or maybe a few days or years and it becomes life. It lives and grows in the deepest shelter of our-self.

Then you breathe; not for the first time but again and again, allowing a great tenderness to open up inside. You let go; knowing that you belong to this time, to each other, to this world and to something that is both within and larger than it all – the one breath. The breath becomes beyond air, it is flesh, blood, bone, salt and tears…

It's… the inside-out pains and joy, life sorrows, betrayals, laughter and screams. It's the pull of the heart or the quickening of the blood that urges us forward and it's the fear of the journey. It's longing larger than fear and the parts of ourselves we ache for and the parts we attempted to leave behind. It's the depression of a downtrodden soul, and the falling and rising again and again. It's skin on skin bliss of first times and the exquisite beauty and the bone-wrenching sorrow of being fully alive. It's the intimacy with self and the world for which our soul hungers. It's the star-exploded night and planets squaring the moon, sunrise, sunset and breaking dawn. It is you; the song of the heart pounding beating drum.

Journal Prompt:

What are the names of the breaths you take, over and over for yourself and others…?

TIME FLIES

*L*ife is short. That is another one of those facts of life you can't escape. It's tick-tocking away. It's precious. Don't go wasting a single minute of it. The happiest people in life are those that extract every last moment of adventure and energy from it. There are areas in life we have control over and a whole lot of areas we don't and we worry. There are lots of ways in life you can make a difference and other ways you can't – let go. If you waste time worrying and struggling to change things/people/stuff that are never going to be changed, then life will fly by, along with a whole host of opportunities and you'll miss it. I worry about lots and lots of things, every time I turn the news on and I see children starving, dying, wars, destruction and all of the terrible reports we see on television, my heart breaks. I want to be able to help everyone and save them all. I want the message to *"Be the Human Sunshine"* to infect every

" If we all came together in the spirit of human sunshine we could change pretty much everything..."

heart and cause an epidemic where no cure is needed. But I am realistic. I know I cannot save and change the world – that is something we hopefully all aspire to do as human beings.

Dedicating your life to the things you can change (you can include this in your mission statement), areas where you can make a difference, then your life becomes happier and more fulfilled. And the happier it is the more time you seem to have. If we all came together in the spirit of human sunshine we could change pretty much everything, but that is a personal statement. You can't change the world but you can change your little corner of it.

Journal Prompt:

How can you change your little corner of the world? (Volunteer, be kinder to people etc.).

TIME FOR REGRETS

*G*ood old regrets… we have all had a few. I know what you are all thinking, "Life is too short – no time for regrets". Think again! Regrets can come in very handy indeed – if you choose to use your regrets wisely and allow them to make a difference in your life as you step forward on your journey for change.

There are many regrets people have, for instance: regrets when you have hurt or been unkind to somebody intentionally/unintentionally, or when you feel you have missed out on life's opportunities (missed the boat) simply because you should've bought a first class ticket aboard the ship of opportunity and adventure. Ask yourself, "How often do I use the word "should" in my daily life?" Have you ever noticed how this word adds to the pressure that you put on yourself? Maybe your inner voice is continually telling you that you "should" have done this or you "should" do that. "Should" implies you could do better or that you might be doing something wrong. Now think of the word "could". This word gives you a choice: it softens the blow of what you need to do. If you eliminate the word "should" and substitute with the word "could" you might feel a lot happier and not so stressed.

Or, if you see others doing well and wish it were you, don't be envious. We see this often don't we and it really is so sad, jealousy is a bitterness of the soul, never give in to jealousy. Use their success as an inspirational tool, let them motivate you. Instead of saying "I should" – replace it with "I could". Make time for your regrets; embrace them all. If you want to feel the sunshine you have to get out of the shade. If you have the chance to make up to somebody what you have done/said – say sorry. Regrets can be quite liberating and freeing. Instead of creating a bucket list create time for a regrets list. You deserve it. Set sail "me-hearties" ride the cosmic waves – the sky isn't the limit it's beyond out into the infinite galaxy and myriad of stars "where moonbeams fall".

Journal Prompt:

List all of your regrets, make time for them then dispose of them into your Pickle Jar.

"TWIT-TWOO"

*D*eep within the inner-self in all of us is a well of wisdom. Wisdom is often born in the shadows, more visible in the darkness than in light. Wisdom is often called intuition and we rarely listen to it. Listening to your intuition is a slow learnt process. It starts by recognising that tiny inner voice or feeling that will tell you when something is wrong or not quite right. It's an incredibly calm, quiet voice and needs silence and focus (mindfulness) to hear it to begin with. We all must move into darker places if we are to find the wisdom we so desperately need. And while we rarely listen, we rarely go there willingly either for the fear of what we are told and for the truth of what we will hear. It is a fact every life contains its own cycles of sorrow and joy. To meet wisdom we must be willing to enter into those darkened places and be willing to hold all of what life has to offer, even if it is something so large we cannot hold it ourselves. Do not fear – we are held.

We often call this inner voice our conscience. The voice or feeling that lets us know right from wrong, good or bad. You know when you've hurt someone, or done something wrong, you know when you have to make amends, put things right.

It's a familiar feeling that you know and it has been with you all of your life. There's no hiding or running away from it.

When you start listening to that inner voice (conscience or gut feeling), you will find it can help you. It will become the wise owl perched on your shoulder, "twit-twooing" away. Listen to the voice within (what is it twit-twelling you?). It helps with the questions, "Why am I doing this/should I do this?" If you listen carefully your wise owl (your inner-self) will answer. You can ask yourself questions when confronted with "Is this a good or bad idea?" or when decision-making, you will find you can answer yourself. And you'll find you already know everything there is to know and everything you'll ever need to know. Nobody knows you better, than you. You have all the facts at hand, all the knowledge deep within your inner well of wisdom, you just need to throw in a penny and bring it to the surface. If you're going to trust anybody to advise or guide you what better person can there be other than yourself? It makes sense for it to be you because you have all the facts, all the experience and knowledge, perched there right on your shoulder – "Twit-twoo – invest in you".

Journal Prompt:

What do you hear when you ask your "wise owl" friend a question – try this several times over the next few weeks. Has it worked for you?

WHAT ECHOES FROM THE TONGUE, ECHOES FROM THE HEART

"SPEAK TRUTH FROM YOUR HEART, HOLD NO SLANDER OR SLURS UPON YOUR TONGUE, DO EACH OTHER NO WRONG. SPEAK ONLY WITH HUMAN SUNSHINE."

SUNSHINE SCROLLS

It's very easy for us to criticise, complain and moan; most of us do it every day. Things get us down whether at home or at work, socially or in society. We find it so much harder to find something nice to say about a situation or a person, it's as if a huge cloud of negativity settles upon our tongue. As humans it's our natural tendency to moan and complain, but sometimes the words we speak are like a *tornado;* they can cause severe distress to others without us even realising. We tend to focus on the things that annoy us or that we don't like about others rather than focusing on their good qualities and attributes. Just imagine if the only words you spoke from your mouth were positive, kind words, how great you would feel. How great you would make others feel.

Think of your words as cloud chasers and every time you said something positive, or gave a compliment you chased the negative clouds away. Think of it as a personal challenge for yourself daily, at home, work or socially. If someone asks you "How was your day?" pick the pieces that you did like about the day, maybe the things that made you smile, or fulfilled you, regardless of whether the rest of your day was crappy. To be a generally happy, positive person can help heal you, even if you're feeling down or suffering yourself. Go on, create a little sunshine effect. I double dare you. It may just come echoing back to you…

Journal Reflection:

Are you a cloud chaser or are you a tornado tongue?

Journal Challenge:

For one week – try thinking before you speak – speak only positive words. You will feel amazing and your mood will shift into a happier place. Write in your journal how you felt and if you helped create a calmer, happier atmosphere.

Journal Prompt:

Are there any relationships you need to heal, maybe because of harsh words that were spoken in an argument? I would like to improve my relationship with (blank) because… What are the main problems? What solutions can you think of? What are some good points to the relationship? For example, at the worst, this relationship may have taught you about how not to treat other people. What would the benefits of this relationship working better be?

Journal Task:

Write a letter to someone you need to forgive or need forgiveness from.

SELF-PROTECT

*O*ften, we can feel quite vulnerable and uneasy; visualise a golden sunbeam surrounding and protecting you on all sides, head to toe. Imagine the sunbeam has a protective layer within its rays. The beautiful golden rays protect you from all that is negative outside of you. However, the sunbeam allows your own love and light to radiate out of it. Keep this image in your mind until you feel the warmth, calmness and peace filling every cell of your body.

Journal Task:

Set a beautiful golden sun in all of its glory as your screensaver on your computer/laptop/phone or device. Or, place a beautiful bunch of sunflowers in your favourite part of the house in a beautiful vase and when you need to be reminded of this calm feeling, to de-stress, look at the image/flowers for five minutes.

Journal Prompt:

Describe your feelings when you look at the image of the sun/sunflowers, do you feel a sense of calm and warmth? What does the sun represent to you?

BE THE CURE

*I*llness isolates; healing restores. Who has not felt his or her spirits lifted during illness by the healing words of a relative or friend? A kind word, or touch in the form of human sunshine can be enough to change our attitude from depression, sadness, sorrow and despair to hope and happiness. In sharing our inner sunbeam we inspire healing and recovery. Our compassionate, caring attitude can be a powerful medicine, pain relief, remedy and in some cases – a cure. When we speak it must be from a caring tongue and open heart. "The heart has its own language – the heart knows a hundred thousand ways to speak – human sunshine is the universal language where no words are needed."

Just think! You can dispense human sunshine and share your inner sunbeam at any time, in any moment wherever you are or go. We are all called into life to be the healers of another. I urge you to be the deepest call for all whose life is the roar of waterfalls, waves and thunder. Be lost in the call.

Journal Prompt:

How can I reach out to someone who is ill or suffering today? How did I feel during illness when somebody had helped care for me? Who was that person/s? What do I feel toward them? How might I become more conscious of the healing that I can bring to others in my family, at work or in my community by simply being present and sharing my inner sunbeam?

Affirmation:

Divine Creator gift me with the healing grace, patience and understanding to bring healing to those who are suffering and in need of human sunshine.

EVERYBODY NEEDS A FRIEND

*L*ist all the friends you are closest to, including those who have been a source of warmth (a sunbeam) in your life. Identify those you like to be closer to on another list. Make a third list of what you would like to talk about, or do, with each of your friends. Is there anyone you would like to call/text/Facebook-poke/ Tweet/email right now?

Journal Prompt:

You can also use one of your closest friends as a "Worry Buster", you can either contact them when you're worried about something, or simply visualise them chasing your cares away.

Journal Challenge:

Is there anybody in your community who is in need of a friend? Think of somebody in the street/area in which you live that is in need of comfort and friendship or a listening ear. What could you do to make a difference in their lives?

OFFER A HELPING HAND

*C*an you remember the last person you helped? What did you do to help them? How did it make you feel when you offered a helping hand? When we help others we actually help ourselves. Acts of kindness and compassion remove us from our own neediness and into someone else's sphere of need. Make it your mission if you have spare time to volunteer, help the homeless, help a neighbour, or somebody in your community, a family member or friend. If someone tells you that a certain person is lost, lonely, miserable or distressed, realise that person is out of tune (out of sorts) and add a little song to their life – hold out your hand, ask them to dance. You never know, one day you may need a little music or helping hand. Be a rainbow in somebody's cloud, show your colours today.

Journal Prompt:

Is there anybody who needs your help? Who are they and why? How do you feel helping them? Could you do with a little help?

IT'S IN THE SMILE

*L*aughter is key: it is a highly effective way of releasing stress and calming you down. Laughter has been proven to lower the blood pressure, reduce stress hormones and boost immune function. Laughter also triggers the release of endorphins and produces a general sense of overall well-being.

"Smiles create such a joy that rekindles the heart, transcending moments of just living. Rare moments where we lose control, reaching heights of such splendour and beauty. Smiles represent the ecstatic rush of finding moments that are real magic."

"Let no one ever come to you without leaving better and happier. Be the living expression of Divine kindness: kindness in your face, kindness in your eyes and kindness in your smile. Be glad you brought a smile because you are a human sunbeam."

Journal Prompt:

When was the last time you laughed so hard your cheeks hurt? Has a stranger ever smiled at you during a day or time when you needed it? How did it make you feel?

Journal Challenge:

Every day offer your smile to every person you meet whether you know them or not. How did it make you feel sharing a smile with somebody you didn't know?

Have you ever stopped to think, "a smile costs nothing, yet means so much". You may be the only friendly smile a person will receive that day. There are so many lonely people in your community/society who are in need of a smile; "curl your lips, it really is infectious" and smile your way to "ha, ha, ha, ha, happy".

Exercise The Mind,
Body And Soul

LITTLE PIECES OF USEFUL
SOMETHING

"Write down all of the calming activities you intend to do..."

This section of the journal sets out simple tasks, activities, affirmations and meditations to accompany your journaling experience. I look upon them as exercises (keep fit) for the mind, body and spirit with intention of emotional and mental wellness and reflection. I have included a variety of prompts, activities and tasks; "I wish I could have included more, but there is always my next book". Use them daily or weekly. By making small daily changes along with your journaling, you can work toward changing the habits of a lifetime that limit you living fully.

Enjoy them – write down all of the calming, stress-reducing activities you have tried or intend to do. You can also add your own. Enjoy! Have fun.

MANTRAS AND AFFIRMATIONS

A mantra is a declaration of something true. It is usually a phrase or sentence, or it can be a single word. In the field of positive thinking and self-development, it is all about fostering a belief of positive mental attitude.

In fact, did you know that the concept of mantras has been around for hundreds, even thousands of years? They were first written about in ancient Vedic scriptures, which went back as old as 1,000 B.C.E. At that time, mantras were simply either words or sounds aimed to be repeated to attain positive changes in life. So, by crafting a positive mantra, you are in effect using something as ancient as time, also tried, tested and proven!

Mantras and affirmations follow a few rules:

Mantras should be short and simple. The mantra may also be in a long sentence, but it must capture the essence and passion of your belief. The mantra should be in the present tense.

Use "I am…", "I have…", "I will…", "I love…" Do not use "I want…" or "I can't…" because you are demonstrating the feelings of desire and lack of belief, not the affirmation of what *is* there.

Use only positive words in your mantras. In creating mantras, if it is a prosperity mantra, you are taking the first step in fulfilling your prosperity goals and your wildest wealth dreams. You will take this step in achieving your abundant wealth success. Let your wealth begin right now by creating your very own prosperity mantra.

Below are some powerful prosperity affirmations, which you can use to create your own wealth and prosperity mantras.

I have been given endless talents, which I begin to utilise today.

I am the architect of my own life; I build its foundation and choose its contents.

I feel good about money and I deserve it in my life.

My thoughts are filled with positivity and my life is plentiful with happiness and prosperity.

The universe has chosen me to be prosperous so I can help humanity with my wealth.

Creative energy surges through me and leads me to new and brilliant ideas.

I prosper wherever I turn on this journey and I know that I deserve prosperity of all kinds.

My future is an ideal projection of what I envision now.

Have fun creating your own mantras and say them aloud to yourself every day. Say them in the morning, at midday, in the evening. Repeat five times at every session.

It may seem a little awkward at first, having to speak your mantras aloud to yourself, but speaking them aloud is the most powerful way you can reinforce the mantra and embed it into your subconscious, especially if you do it with the fullest conviction, positive energy and belief.

Write your mantras on cards, or reminders, gadgets or gizmos, put them everywhere that your attention falls. As I have previously written; speak aloud, visualise your success, believe it, because it has happened.

As you see your affirmation manifest, whether big or small, repeat your mantra in your mind. I call this "mantra maintenance", maintaining repetitive positivity is essential, enabling you to make a tight connection between your subconscious mind and your mantra, linking both together. Remember like attracts like, that's the Law of Attraction. Happiness and prosperity is a part of your life, create your mantras and make it so.

"Wave your wand over your mantras if you wish to, a little extra magic will do no harm."

CHAKRA TABLE

VIOLET/PURPLE:

governs the CROWN chakra, at the top of the head.

Beauty, Creativity, Inspiration

INDIGO:

governs the BROW chakra or third eye, in the centre of the forehead.

Intuition, Mysticism, Understanding

BLUE:

governs the THROAT chakra.

Knowledge, Health, Decisiveness

GREEN:

governs the HEART chakra.

Balance, Love, Self-Control

YELLOW:

governs the SOLAR PLEXUS chakra, situated below the ribs.

Wisdom, Clarity, Self-Esteem

ORANGE:

governs the SACRAL chakra, situated in the lower abdomen.

Happiness, Confidence, Resourcefulness

RED:

governs the BASE chakra, situated at the base of the spine.

Vitality, Courage, Self-Confidence

GO POTTY AND LOSE THE PLOT EVERY NOW AND AGAIN!

"*G*oing Potty" every once in a while is a real chill-out experience. Plants that you grow and nurture yourself are truly calming; pottering around your own garden is a relaxing experience. Don't worry if you don't have a garden, visit a garden centre or nursery, or get some beautiful indoor plants to put in a window box – create your own little life garden, pick plants and colours that represent you.

Or you can create your own chakra garden – your garden can be created anywhere indoors or outdoors. If you are creating an indoor garden I recommend you purchase a beautiful, ceramic coloured window pot to place your indoor plants in. The coloured flowers you choose should represent the colour of the chakras and should be potted in colour order.

Place your potted chakra garden in the space where you write and complete the Rainbow Effect Meditation (on following pages) to bring balance to chakras before journaling.

Journal Task:

Take a picture of your garden and stick it in your journal.

A LITTLE RAINBOW EFFECT
MEDITATION

*S*it or lie comfortably, relax your entire body, close your eyes and take a few deep breaths. Imagine a beautiful rainbow settling over your entire body and mentally scan one particular muscle as you inhale. As you exhale, imagine the beautiful vibrant colours releasing all of the tension as the muscle relaxes.

Then, systematically scan your entire body, begin at the top of your head and work down to your face, eyes, jaw, neck, shoulders, arms, hands, back, thighs, legs and feet. For each tight, stressed area, mentally repeat the following: "beautiful rainbow I feel all of your vibrant colours flowing into every part of my… heal me." If your mind gets lost on a cloud somewhere, just bring your attention back to the colours of the rainbow and continue scanning your body until you feel completely relaxed. We all need a "little rainbow effect" every now and again.

Journal Prompt:

What feelings did you experience during this meditation?

ART THERAPY JOURNALING

*U*sing drawing, painting or fabrics in your journaling as a release from stress or tension isn't about talent or technique. It's about using colour, doodling, jottings, textures and shapes.

You may like to use crayons, felt-tips, pencils or paints and you might want to use craft items such as glitter, stars, coloured paper, ribbon, luggage labels or pipe-cleaners etc.

Creating art journal pages in your journal is extremely therapeutic. Art is used in various homeless hostels, hospitals, prisons, schools and rehabilitation centres around the world to help overcome certain events and life traumas that people have experienced.

Journal Task:

Create art journaling pages throughout your journal; let your pictures tell a story. Spontaneously start drawing, letting your hand move wherever it wants to go.

Take a photograph of your favourite journal page and paste it into your journal.

*F*ind a quiet place, lie or sit down, close your eyes and take in a deep breath. Become aware of the need for something else: for the wisdom to live with what you do not know, what you cannot control, what is painful and still choose life. Give yourself permission to "let go of the hurt, the pain and control". Repeat silently to yourself several times, "I am letting go of all of the control and the pain." Every time you exhale, imagine you are cleansing your mind of all the clutter and control that you don't need, leaving you so relaxed and so much happier than before.

Journal Prompt:

What "excess baggage" are you carrying around? Create a list of all the negative things you would like to drop off at lost property, such as a regret, a negative self-belief or a past event; tell me how releasing them would make you feel.

What are you dwelling on from your past that prevents you from moving forward? Put all of your dwellings into your "Pickle Jar".

SURRENDER

*S*urrendering is one of the most positive, liberating words in the English language. Think about what this word means and contemplate it fully. To surrender does not only mean to give up: to surrender to the day means – have no expectations or preconceived ideas of what the day will bring. Expecting things in a certain way prevents you from feeling, seeing and appreciating what is and can be, surrendering means to be free of limitations – to accept all that comes your way as part of the adventure of being fully alive.

Surrender your fixed expectations today, observe and appreciate all of the wonderful things that you will encounter when least expected.

Journal Prompt:

What/who will you surrender to today?

WORRY BUSTER

SAINT CHRISTOPHER GUIDE AND PROTECT ME
AS I TRAVEL THE ROADS OF LIFE.

*I*f you are a "worry wart" and worry won't leave you alone, use a wonderful technique I use called "Worry Buster". Sit down for a few moments and imagine yourself calling in your "Worry Buster". Close your eyes and say to yourself silently and peacefully, "I will not allow worries to cloud up my thoughts today. Worry Busters – chase my cares away." Visualise the Worry Busters chasing all of the worrying thoughts out of your mind.

Journal Prompt:

The next time you feel those worrying thoughts popping into your head – "Who are you going to call?"

DAY DREAM BELIEVER

*T*his is a really important rule in the life of a journal keeper: "DAY DREAM BELIEVER – DARE TO DREAM". You would be surprised how many people limit their dreams. They are your dreams and there should be no limit to what you dream for. You are allowed to dream as extravagant, as impossible, as unusual, as fantastic or off the wall as you want. Dreams are limitless.

You are all allowed to wish for anything too. They are your wishes and dreams and they are a private thing between you and your journal and no one else at all.

I must warn you – I do speak from personal experience – this book is testimony, be careful what you dream for because it might just come true. What would you do then?

People think their dreams have to be sensible or credible to be worthy of dreaming about. But that's a goal and that is something totally different. Goals require planning and small steps to make them materialise, you have all heard of SMART targets – small, measurable, achievable, realistic, and timely. There is nothing small about a dream and there are no limits, no boundaries and no time restrictions. If you are going to dream you may as well dream BIG. Just remember the most successful people in life are those who were "DAY DREAM BELIEVERS or DOLLY DAY-DREAMS" but they are also the people who were not afraid to DARE to DREAM. Always remember if you can dream it, you can do it. My dream started with a pen and a blank page.

Journal Prompt:

What do you dream of doing with your life? Is there anything/anyone preventing you from achieving your dreams? Flick back to the "Journ – Map" page for reflection. Take action.

RIPPLE EFFECT

*A*s you go forward into life please remember, in sharing our human sunbeam we are like a tiny pebble dropped into the ocean, the effects of what we do ripples outwardly in increasingly wider circles. Through the power of the sunbeam, the little ways in which we deliver human sunshine through an open heart, empathy, love, goodness, kindness, forgiveness, tolerance, patience, selflessness, and compassion ripple out, further than we can imagine.

Love and compassion are the ultimate source of human happiness, and the very need for them both lies at the very core of our being. In creating this ripple effect you will have a happy home, family, friendships and relationships. Happiness comes from an open heart and forgiveness. Happiness cannot come from hatred or anger – happy you, happy people, happy world.

THE WISHING TREE

*T*he wishing tree is originally a Dutch wedding tradition. Each guest is given a piece of card or a manila tag to write a message on for the bride and groom, then they hang it on the tree. As guests write their messages the tree fills up with beautiful leaves of warm wishes. The tree makes a beautiful center piece and can be placed anywhere around the reception area. After the wedding the wishes are taken off and placed in a *memory box* for safekeeping and *good luck*. The tree can be used as a decoration or ornament.

A wishing tree can also be used for other occasions: birthdays, graduation, Christmas, New Year resolutions or simply for inspiration. I create a wishing tree for Christmas and New Year and hang all of my hopes, dreams and wishes for my family, friends and those I feel need a little extra help as well as myself on it. I also ask every visitor who comes to my home to add their wishes to my wishing tree, it is essential you don't wish for yourself alone. I decorate the tree with beautiful coloured ribbon and pieces that have inspired me: poetry, quotes, images, photographs and angel images, adding messages to it when I need to. I send out all of my wishes into the universe and into heaven, holding faith all of the messages will be listened to. I leave the tree up all year round and remove those wishes that have come true from it into a decorated memory box. Those wishes that have yet to come true stay on the branches until they do. Sitting under your very own wishing tree is the perfect place to have your Juliet Date.

Journal Challenge:

Create your own wishing tree, write out your messages on manila tags and hang them onto the branches.

You can find wishing trees online, or purchase a pre-lit twig tree; the lights add a little extra sparkle to the wishes and look beautiful in the evening dimly lit.

Sunshine
In A Pocket

"ALL THE THINGS I NEVER SAID"

Even though we make a point to regularly tell our family and friends how much they mean to us, when a loved one dies, especially when it is sudden and unexpected, we wish we could tell them we love them just one more time. We yearn desperately for one more conversation with them, one more gesture of love from them that will help us to say goodbye and offer healing, closure and removal of guilt. Guilt is one of the hardest parts we have to deal with when a loved one dies. We start blaming ourselves: "if only I had of done this/that or I could have/should have done more" etc.

You have the power and the opportunity to comfort your loved ones and ease their grief when death comes a calling. (It is going to happen to all of us.) How? Write a letter now and label it *"Open this letter in the event of my death"*. I have written such a letter to my children, and have told them where they can find it and my journal should the day come when it is time for them to read it.

Imagine your loved one opening and reading your letter after your passing. The gratitude, love and peace of mind your letter will bestow upon them is more valuable than any earthly possession. They will cherish that letter as long as they live, just as they will cherish the very thought of you.

Your letter can be as long or as short as you'd like; even a few sentences can have an enormous impact. The quality of the writing is irrelevant. All that matters is the love behind the words; write from your heart and you cannot go wrong. There is no greater gift you can bequeath to those you love.

You can use ribbon to seal the pocket in your journal by simply hole punching the paper or you can use your own wax seal. Personalised wax seal kits can be found online.

Journal Prompt:

Tell me about someone you miss. Either someone who passed away, moved or you have simply drifted apart from.

What experiences did you share? How did they make you feel? What did you learn from them?

Who is or was your human sunshine? Paste a photograph in your journal. Let this picture inspire you as you move forward into life.

Write a letter to someone who believed in you even when you didn't believe in yourself.

GOODBYE, ADIOS, SAYONARA

*A*DIOS, SAYONARA. Write out your own ideal obituary for when you are really old and have peacefully passed away in your sleep. Your success or failure in life will be reflected on your obituary unless someone manipulates the truth on your behalf. Writing your own private obituary is an out of the box way of thinking about your life and what you call success.

It is an excellent way to put your life into perspective and I recommend that you try it. Many people would rather not think about it. There is comfort in not thinking about death. It is a taboo subject. But given a long enough timeline we shall all cease to exist. Why not use this taboo subject to change the course of your destiny and improve the days and years ahead?

Journal Prompts:

Who do you want to be dearly missed by? What do you want to be remembered for? What do you want your list of achievements to have been?

Imagine you could oversee your funeral, what would you want to hear people saying about you?

What would your epitaph be?

QUALITIES OF HUMAN SUNSHINE

*S*ome humans (*Mother Teresa, Malala Yousafzai, Nelson Mandela amongst others*) have become identified with particular endearing and enduring qualities, reflecting a range of attributes toward which we can only aspire. Each one of us, wherever we are on our individual spiritual paths, can be inspired by the everyday gift of human sunshine. Below, I describe human sunshine qualities and encourage you to develop each one in yourself.

Humility: Act out the Divine will of the Beloved, Divine Creator and care for humankind. While we live in a competitive world, humility might seem unfashionable, perhaps a weakness or a reflection of low self-esteem. To be humble is not the same as being submissive, to be humble means to act selflessly, to practice the acceptance of diversity and its many, many challenges, and to cultivate the spirit of service and deliver human sunshine to those around us. There is beauty in the gesture to *deliver human sunshine* and be of *service to others*, the gesture of total acceptance of each other and the world is an inspiration in itself.

Service: To *Be the Human Sunshine* and of *service to others* "how beautiful is that, it really is quite something isn't it, don't you think?" To exist to serve God, the Beloved, Divine Creator (or that/which/who you have faith or belief in) and humankind offers great comfort to us, not to mention a valuable pattern of behaviour of which others can observe, learn and grow from. And whilst I state in the *Morning Journaling* piece we never get time entirely for ourselves, and even in the *alone time* we spend most of it worrying about others, sometimes we have to be a *little selfish* – do not confuse this message. We of course have to look after ourselves, allowing time for self-nurturing. If we do not take care of ourselves, how can we take care of others? Ideally, we aim to make some self-sacrifices for others without relinquishing our personal goals or dreams. But I too am realistic that our responsibilities and commitment to others sometimes puts a hold on our dreams; if our loved ones or those that we are responsible for fall ill or are going through a tough time, dreams then seem unimportant. Our *selfish me time* once again turns into selflessness, we are only human.

We can all earn spiritual credit by selflessness. The law of Karma clearly dictates, as well as many other spiritual guidebooks written by many great authors, philosophers past and present: acts of loving service will bring back similar blessings to those who initiate them. But! Do we humans need some great philosopher to tell us the law of the heart, the law of life? The meaning of life. Is it not basic common sense? A learned behaviour we individually can teach each other regardless of religion, ethnicity, faith or belief. Some people have no teacher, but all humans can be taught to open the sun of the heart. We all have a duty to each-other to share our inner sunbeam and deliver human sunshine. Emulate Mother Teresa, Malala Yousafzai, Nelson Mandela or those you aspire to by offering to serve any person/ group who are oppressed, disadvantaged or in need. I *promise you* your sense of self-worth will increase immensely. Take some time to consider the lives you have touched, have gratitude for those that have shown you human sunshine and then share *your* inner sunbeam. Infect others. Be mindful, begin with your own home and those around you; *be their teacher.* You don't need to go to a remote place to make a difference. Start with your own home and community. Also, you don't need to make huge sacrifices or give money "*true wealth is not determined in the form of paper and coins alone*"; learn to contribute with your heart not just your pocket. If nothing else, just spend a bit of time with those that are lonely and alone.

Have a solid foundation in which those close to you and around you can build upon, allow your core values of love and wanting to serve others keep you going when faced with the turmoil and challenges of life – keep the faith, faith in you. You can make a difference.

Journal Prompts:

What are your core beliefs and values? What will you never compromise on? And if you were to follow the path set by those you aspire to, what would you do?

Create a following: Lead by example, once you are aligned to a great cause or particular calling and you have a core foundation, you would do well to create a following as it's more fashionably described nowadays on Twitter. Part of creating a following is to be media savvy and many great philanthropists have capitalized on any opportunity to promote a cause and to raise funds. Just think what many of those we aspire to in the past would have done with all of the social media tools at their behest today! They would have added friends, poked, hashtagged and tweeted all day long if they thought it would have made a difference.

Ride the storm: Throughout your life, you too may face some challenges to your authority and integrity. You must learn to look through people's hidden agendas and remain true to your cause, ride the storm and remain committed to your faith and intentions. If need be, take time out for yourself and reaffirm that you are truly on your chosen path. It's also okay to change course if it feels like the right thing to do – consult your *journ-map* if necessary and create a new plan of action.

Open your heart; share your inner sunbeam: Allow your innermost endearing and enduring qualities to shine through, infect all with your human sunshine and keep smiling and loving with an open heart, one filled with love, respect, dignity and compassion even when faced with the harshest of challenges. Remember! If you come from a place of love and with a mindset of helping, then somehow you will find the ability and internal resources to do so.

149

Somehow; things will work out for you just fine. There is no greater gift to give other than yourself, the gift of *human sunshine*.

Journal Prompt:

How can you share your inner sunbeam and spread this loving message of *Be the Human Sunshine* around the world in whatever way large or small or in a way that feels right to you?

*

In the beginning we all depend on *love* and *affection* from our mother, father or guardians.

Without loving care we cannot survive.

Without loving action *we miss the meaning of life*.

Give all of you with an open heart and expect

nothing in return, do the ordinary, simple things

with extraordinary love.

Be the Human Sunshine.

*

STATEMENT OF
BE THE HUMAN SUNSHINE

*L*ive your life with steadfast faith, faith in the Divine Creator – the Mystery – faith in you.

Allow only those thoughts to enter your mind that are inspiring from above and within.

Share your inner sunbeam, spread human sunshine wherever you go, and in the knowing the Divine walks with you.

Give the very best of you, love because you are at peace with loving – expect nothing in return.

Love all like the Divine loves with a deep soul–filled love, humankind, nature, all creatures, animals and flying birds remembering they too are the living song – understand their tongues.

Have faith, ask and you shall receive, pray for every living thing not yourself alone.

Live in perpetual gratitude to the Divine for the privilege of living, life is a privilege, a gift.

All answers will be given in time, and in the knowing that having faith is just enough.

Let us all make life beautiful simply by being human.

BE THE HUMAN SUNSHINE

*A*s we say "goodbye" I shall leave you with a statement to hold on to (if you remember I said at the beginning of the book, I shall save for the end of the book) here goes.

"As you continue on your journaling experience of enlightenment there is only one destination you need to get to, that place is to journey home to yourself; you are a volume in the Divine book, a mirror to the power that created the universe. Whatever you want ask of it yourself, whatever you are journeying or searching for can only be found inside of you."

I live in hope that all roots of suffering diminish, may you all find your inner sunbeam, and as we deliver human sunshine together may violence, warfare, indifference, oppression, addiction, homelessness, hunger and poverty decrease. May compassion and forgiveness be cultivated from the wisdom and awareness of all suffering, may you continue to open your hearts and minds in order to work tirelessly for the benefit of all human beings.

Share your inner sunbeam and
Be The Human Sunshine,

Wees die Human Sunshine,
BëhuSunshine Njerëzore,
الـشمس المشـرقـة الإنـسان
كـن,
Եղեք մարդու Sunshine,
Yeghek' mardu **Sunshine,**
Ýnsan Sunshine olun,
Kontuz Giza Sunshine,
Будзьце Human **Саншайн,**
Budźcie Human Sanšajn,
হউিম্যান র·দ করা,
Hi'umyâna rôda karâ,
Budite Human Sunshine,
Бъдете Human Sunshine,
Bŭdete Human Sunshine,
Sigues el Sol Humà,
Himoa nga ang Human
Sunshine,
是人类阳光,
Shì rénlèi yángguāng,
是人類陽光,
Shì rénlèi yángguāng,
BuditeHuman Sunshine,

BuďteHuman Sunshine,
Bliv den menneskelige
Sunshine,
Schrijf Human Sunshine,
Estu la Homaj Sunshine,
Maging ang Human Sunshine,
Ole Human Sunshine,
Soyez le Soleil humain,
იყოს ადამიანის
Sunshine,
iqos adamianis Sunshine,
Schreiben Sie die Menschen
Sonnenschein,
Είναι το ανθρώπινο
Sunshine,
Eínai to anthrópino Sunshine,
હ્યુમન સનશાઈન હોઈ,
Hyumana sanaûâ'ina hô'î,
Fè Sunshine nan Imèn,
Zama Human Sunshine,
להיותSunshine האדם,
मानव सनशाइन रहो,
Mānava sanaśā'ina rahō,

Yog tus tib neeg Sunshine,
Legyél te az Emberi Napfény,
Vertu Human Sunshine,
Ịbụ Human Sunshine,
Jadilah Sunshine Manusia,
Bí ar an Sunshine Daonna,
Diventa il sole umano,
人間のサンシャインて,
Ningen no Sanshainte,
Dadi Sunshine Human,
ಮಾನವ ಸನ್ಶೈ್ನ ಎಂದು,
Mānava sanśain endu,
ជា មនុស្ស ពន្លឺថ្ងៃ,
chea mnoussa ponlu th,
인간 선샤인 한다,
ingan seonsyain handa,
ເປັນ ແຊງຕາ Sunshine,
pen manud Sunshine,
Esto Humanum Sunshine,
EsiHuman Sunshine,
BūkiteŽmogaus Sunshine,
Биди човекови Сонце,
Bidi čovekovi Sonce,
Menjadi Sunshine Manusia,
Kun l- Sunshine Bniedem,
Kia te Human Sunshine,
मानवी सुर्यप्रकाश व्हा,
Mânavî suryaprakâúa vhâ,
Хүний Sunshine байх,

Khünii Sunshine baikh,
मानव घाम हुनुहोस्,
Mānava ghāma hunuhōs,
Bli den menneskelige Sunshine,
باشیی آفتاب بشـر,
BądźSunshine Ludzki,
Seja o sol Humano,
ਮਨੁੱਖੀ ਸਨਸ਼੍ਹਾਇਨ ਰਹੋ,
Manukhī sanśhā'ina rahō,
Fii Sunshine uman,
БудьтеHuman Саншайн,
Bud'te Human Sanshayn,
Будите људска Сунсхине,
Budite ljudska Sunshine,
Buďte Human Sunshine,
BoditeHuman Sunshine,
Noqo Sunshine Insaanka,
Sé el Sol Humano,
Kuwa Sunshine Binadamu,
Var Human Sunshine,
மனித சன்ஷைன் இருங்கள்,
Maṉita caṉṣaiṉ iruṅkaḷ,

,
Mānava sanṣain uṇḍaṇḍi,
เป็นซันไชน์ ของมนุษย์,
Pĕn saṇ chiṇˈ khxng mnusˈyˈ,
Ínsan Sunshine Be,
Будьте Human Саншайн,

Bud'te Human Sanshayn,
انـــسانى ســنشائـــن ,
Hãy là ngýời Sunshine Nhân,
Byddwch y Sunshine Dynol,
מענטשנרעכט סאַנשײן
,זײט די
Zyyt dy m'ntṣnr'kt s'anṣyyn,
Ję awọn Human Sunshine,
Iba Sunshine Human

Remember; regardless of our religion, faith, beliefs, cultural systems or world view "the human sunshine we share is the universal cord of love."

Love
   Clare

Josephine Wall

Iris – Keeper of the Rainbow

The young maiden explores a mysterious wood. Her journey, accompanied by her winged companions leads her towards a portal to a beautiful world. The mellifluous voice of the Goddess welcomes her to this enchanted land, with colourful trees and flowers. A pathway to a land, which seems full of colour and light, compared with the grey cold world through which she has travelled.

Josephine Wall

The Untold Story

As the planet evolves, humankind increasingly leaves the cities to seek peace and consolation in the country. There nature awaits with all her gentleness and beauty to welcome humanity into a more fulfilling way of life.

Josephine Wall

Calling

The young maiden explores a mysterious wood. Her journey, accompanied by her winged companions leads her towards a portal to a beautiful world. The mellifluous voice of the Goddess welcomes her to this enchanted land, with colourful trees and flowers. A pathway to a land, which seems full of colour and light, compared with the grey cold world through which she has travelled.

Josephine Wall

Flora

Wherever Flora, the Roman goddess of flowers, goes, blossoms burst open in a profusion of colourful petals. Her quiet radiance attracts the butterflies while fairies peep through the array of "Flora" that frame her gentle beauty.

Josephine Wall

Moon Goddess

Draped in her glimmering veil of stars, the Goddess Selene tenderly guides the moon on its celestial journey, keeping watch over the night-bathed earth. Her face is lit by the gentle glow of moonbeams from the heavens and by the profound power of her own inner peace and love for mankind.

Josephine Wall

Lighting the Way

"Let us be called to make life beautiful, simply, by being human."

Clare Bostock

Hope Springs Eternal

An angel's loving hand directs a rainbow of hope towards a fertile and beautiful earth, and like a bulb in spring life bursts forth – another gem in the vast garden of the universe.

Josephine Wall

Up, Up and Away

High above the countryside a curious fairy, with a desire to find out what lies beyond her woodland home, is being towed by her butterfly playmates. To her delight she finds that with their help she can fly even higher than her tiny wings would allow. Their wings beat in unison, and gently take her to many far off lands.

Josephine Wall

Sadness of Gaia

The Earth Goddess looks on sadly, aware that our human weaknesses will mean many years of education to prevent the ruin of our precious world. The contents of her wings symbolise all the creatures that need protection. As always "Gaia" will be there to listen and to comfort, bringing with her the rainbow of hope. The clouds are gathering around our world but she knows she must be strong and work to rectify man's errors, in the belief that he will one day understand that our precious earth deserves our protection. Let us hope that one day soon "Gaia" will look upon the earth and be satisfied that her lessons have been learnt!

Josephine Wall

Masque of Love

Having danced the night away she can pretend no more. Struck by Cupids arrow she coyly comes out from behind her mask of peacock feathers to reveal herself for the first time to her masked partner. Having only been able to look into each-other's eyes (the windows of the soul) she knows their feelings for each other are true, and uncomplicated by physical appearance. How can she resist when surrounded by the hypnotic perfume of love.

Josephine Wall

The Phoenix

Rising majestically from the flames this colourful and proud Phoenix embarks on his journey through the world. As he will live for 500 years or more he will travel to all corners of the earth and see many wonderful sights before returning to his nest to be consumed by fire and be re-born to continue his journey.

Josephine Wall

Waiting

In the land of the midnight water lily, the maiden eagerly awaits the arrival of a mysterious galleon. As it enters the flower-lit bay she wonders what bounty it carries. Will it be laden with exotic gifts from a far off land, or maybe this time a gallant lover to whisk her away to faraway places for adventures untold. How long has she been waiting for this moment? In her world time has no meaning, it may have been minutes or years..!!

Josephine Wall

Echoes

"Speak truth from your heart, hold no slander or slurs upon your tongue, do each-other no wrong speak only with human sunshine. A mountain keeps an echo deep inside that is how I hold your voice."

Clare Bostock

The Dryad and the Dragon

Hidden away from prying eyes and deep in a colourful forest, these two magical beings are enjoying getting to know each other. Resting in her roots the young dragon shows no fear of the Willow Dryad as she offers him an exotic fruit, and in return the Dryad feels very safe with her scaly companion. She hopes that they will become friends forever, and that he will visit her often with tales of the world outside of her forest realm.

Josephine Wall

Ripples

As you go forward into life please remember, in sharing our inner sunbeam we are like a tiny pebble dropped into the ocean, the effects of what we do ripples outwardly in increasingly wider circles. Through the power of the sunbeam, the little ways in which we deliver human sunshine through an open heart, empathy, love, goodness, kindness, forgiveness, tolerance, patience, selflessness, and compassion ripple out, further than we can imagine.

Clare Bostock

The Journey

An angel journeys through the universe on her trusty steed, bringing hope and healing to a world beset with problems. The blindfold allows her to focus on how she can help us to become one with nature, and appreciate all the beauty that surrounds us. Cradled in her arms is the epitome of perfection, a rose, which symbolises the ultimate in floral beauty. Each petal contains more love than a thousand words!

Josephine Wall